=== THE ===

PROVING GROUND

NINE TESTS THAT PROVE
YOUR PERSONAL POTENTIAL

KEVIN GERALD

insight
PUBLISHING GROUP

Tulsa, Oklahoma

THE PROVING GROUND

The Proving Ground by Kevin Gerald
Published by Insight Publishing Group
8801 S. Yale, Suite 410
Tulsa, OK 74137
918-493-1718

Unless otherwise noted, Scripture quotations are from the Holy Bible, New International Version, copyright © 1973, 1978, 1984 by International Bible Society. Passages marked KJV are from the King James Version.

ISBN: 1-930027-95-8
Library of Congress catalog card number: 2003102783

Printed in the United States of America

Cover design by:
Rusty George Design
917 Pacific Ave., Suite 607
Tacoma, WA 98402
Telephone: 253.284.2140
Fax: 253.284.2142
Email: info@rustygeorge.com
Web Site: www.rustygeorge.com

Blessed is the man who perseveres under trial, because when he has stood the test, he will receive the crown of life that God has promised to those who love him.

James 1:12

CONTENTS

INTRODUCTION

—— CHAPTER 1 ——

THE TEST OF SMALL THINGS

17

—— CHAPTER 2 ——

THE MOTIVATION TEST

29

—— CHAPTER 3 ——

THE CREDIBILITY TEST

43

—— CHAPTER 4 ——

THE WILDERNESS TEST

59

—— CHAPTER 5 ——

THE AUTHORITY TEST

71

—— CHAPTER 6 ——

THE WARFARE TEST

83

—— **CHAPTER 7** ——

THE OFFENSE TEST
93

—— **CHAPTER 8** ——

THE TEST OF TIME
103

—— **CHAPTER 9** ——

THE LORDSHIP TEST
113

SPECIAL THANKS TO:

My parents, who equipped me for the test

My wife, who is still helping my "scores"on the test…

My daughter, who makes passing the test
more worthwhile

My staff, who I can count on to remind me,
"This is only a test"

INTRODUCTION

THE PROVING OF OUR POTENTIAL

The goal for every achiever is to pass the test. Testing always precedes promotion. If you want to advance to the third grade in school, you must first pass the test of second grade. Likewise, you can't get into college without a high school diploma or equivalent.

Life is similar. God will require each of us to prove our potential at one level before being promoted to the next. When man attempts to be elevated beyond his potential, failure is inevitable. *Self-promotion and human promotion can never replace divine promotion*. Divine promotion only comes through the "proving" of one's personal potential. It is not based upon favoritism or prejudice. It's based totally on what God observes of our conduct and behavior through each test in our lives.

Recognizing a Test

A colorful pattern appears on the TV set, accompanied by a chilling, high-pitched sound. After getting everyone's attention, the announcer verifies that, "This has been a test of the Emergency Broadcast System. I repeat, this is only a test."

Wouldn't it be helpful if the trials in our life were preceded by the announcement, "This is only a test, brought to you by the Heavenly Development System?" The challenge of life's tests is that they often catch us off guard. We're usually not expecting them when they come. If we are alert, the test will come in disguise, so that we don't recognize it. This lack of recognition is one reason many people don't pass the test. My hope is that this book will provide insight to help you better recognize and identify the times of testing in your life. There will never be an announcement, but if we increase our awareness, we can remind ourselves and others that "this is only a test."

The Proving of Your Personal Potential

Our personal potential is unknown until it is proven. In an effort to prepare you for this time of testing, I am going to share with you what I believe are nine of the most common tests that a person experiences. Let's take a brief look at tests that we will be discussing in detail in later chapters.

1. The Test of Small Things
The Test of Small Things comes to prove our potential for opportunities.

2. The Motivation Test
The Motivation Test comes upon a person who is doing the right thing to prove *why* they are doing *what* they are doing.

3. The Credibility Test
The Credibility Test will prove that you maintain integrity, refusing to compromise ethics and morals, in pressured circumstances.

4. The Wilderness Test
The Wilderness Test comes in the form of a drought or dry season. This test will prove your potential to make the changes necessary to enter the next level of maturity and prosperity in your life.

5. The Authority Test
The Authority Test comes to prove your attitude towards the authority that God has put in your life.

6. The Warfare Test
The Warfare Test occurs when you are in the will of God and are experiencing problems. This test will prove how you respond to adversity.

7. The Offense Test
The Offense Test will come to prove that you are not easily offended and that you have the potential to readily forgive others.

8. The Test of Time
The Test of Time comes to prove the quality of your patience and your confidence in God through the seasons in your life.

9. The Lordship Test
The Lordship Test will put you in a position or a situation where it is not easy to obey God. This test is designed to prove if you will obey God's Word and God's will, even when it is not the easy thing to do.

Before you purchase an automobile, it undergoes testing. It must pass these tests before it is declared safe and reliable. In fact, when you get ready to buy a new car, one of the things you want to do, as a wise investor, is to go on a "test drive." In that test drive, you will find out several things: what the car feels like when you steer it, if all the gadgets work, and perhaps even how fast it goes (within the speed limit, of course!). You do all of this to find out if the car is right for you. You test it before you buy it.

Likewise, the food that we eat gets tested. Appliances have a label with a certification number on them that verifies that they have been tested. Aren't you glad that airplanes go through an extensive testing process before you get in them? Airplanes must meet regulations before they can fly. The purpose of testing, in the fashion that I've described to you, is to prove the product. So, the milk we drink, the automobiles we drive, the airplanes we fly in and many other products that we use are all tested to prove their safety and reliability. They are all tested before the consumer is able to purchase, own or use the product. If the product can withstand the test, then the product is declared "user worthy." Only then is it safe to use.

No one wants to have their microwave explode when they push the "start" button. Who would want to turn on a blow-dryer only to discover it's a blowtorch?! The reason the manufacturer can guarantee that something like that will not happen is because they have confirmed, through a testing process, that the product is safe.

In a similar fashion, human beings go through tests in life that determine who we are, what kind of character we have, what we can endure, how dependable and reliable we are, what "temperature" causes us to "melt" and so forth. Who you are and what you are made of—in other words, your "personal potential"—is only proven by testing.

The Difference between Temptation and Testing

Some people picture God dreaming up all kinds of schemes to tempt human beings and then sitting back in his comfortable recliner throne, watching and saying things like, "Bet you don't make this one! Let's see if you can handle that one!" as if, being God, he gets some kind of "high" out of watching mortals being stretched, pushed, tried and tested. That is a wrong concept of God. That is not why we have tests in life.

> *No one should say, 'God is tempting me.' For God cannot be tempted by evil nor does he tempt anyone. But, each one is tempted when by his own evil desire he is dragged away and enticed. After desire has conceived, it gives birth to sin, and sin when it is full-grown, gives birth to death. Do not be deceived. Every good and perfect gift is from above. It comes down from the Father of the heavenly lights, who does not change like shifting shadows.*
>
> James 1:13-17

So, God cannot be tempted by evil, nor does God tempt any man with evil. There is a difference between temptation and testing. I want to help you understand where temptation comes from and where testing comes from. If you really grasp hold of this subject, it will help you through the tests of life, which you'll inevitably encounter.

Let me say again that a test is different than a temptation. For example, when you learn something in school, the test comes to prove what you have learned and is very valuable. A temptation, on the other hand, is not primarily intended to prove what you have learned. A temptation is a device of Satan to entice you to sin.

Have you ever heard people who were going through a difficult time in their life say something like, "The Lord did this to me," or "The Lord tempted me"? That simply isn't true, because the Lord is not capable of originating, instigating or strategizing any kind of evil to tempt you in your life. The Scripture above should make it very clear that God will never tempt any man with sin.

Sin never originates with God. Rather, all evil originates in strategies of Satan. All temptation comes from your enemy. He is the one who devises, the one who strategizes, the one who plots against you to cause you to sin. Satan will challenge every positive claim that you make in your life. So, if you claim to be strong, Satan will see to it that you have to prove it!

Just prior to Jesus entering into public ministry, He was tempted by the devil. In Matthew 4:1-11 you can follow the sequence of events that surrounded Jesus in His hour of temptation. The important point I want you to get, however, is that this time of temptation has its strategic origin in the destructive mind of Satan. God was not tempting Jesus to break His fast, jump from the temple roof or bow down and worship Satan. Moreover, Jesus, when tempted, used resources available to each one of us with which to resist temptation. As the Son of God, He could have played divine power, but instead chose to use the weapon we would use in future times. That weapon is none other than the "Sword of the Spirit," or the spoken word of God. It did not fail Him and it will not fail you.

A Temptation Can Also Be a Test

Although temptation does not come from God, he will allow temptation and use it as a test to prove us. God himself is involved in the process. First, He grants permission for you to be tried. You will not be tried or tested, as a child of God, without God permitting it to be done. Then, God will observe you during the process of your testing. God will watch so that he can prove you. God takes a temptation, and in His eyes, sees it as a test to prove what you can handle—what you are capable of. During God's observation, He is able to determine your potential and your personal ability. He then knows that when He pushes the "start" button on you, you are not going to blow up on Him. *You see, God wants to use you without losing you.* I have never created hardship for my daughter, Jodi. However, there have been times when I chose to not shield her from it. In those times, I observe her closely and am right there "coaching" her all the way. My goal is to see her matured by the hardship. I definitely do not want her to be overwhelmed or damaged. I want to see her made stronger by what she faces and conquers.

Likewise, God is not the creator of the hardships that we face. Sometimes, however, He will choose to not shield us from it and allow the temptation to also be a test, providing us with the opportunity to prove our potential.

God Needs to Verify That You Are "User-Friendly"

Do you remember the burning bush? In the book of Exodus, Moses looked into a burning bush that was ablaze with fire! God was using that bush. Do you know what condition that bush was in when God was through using it? It wasn't burnt up or consumed. It wasn't destroyed. When God was through using it, it returned right back to perfect health.

That's what God wants to do with you and I. He doesn't want to use you at the risk of losing you; He wants to use you without destroying you. He wants to know that when He uses you, you will be able to take it, and He wants to know that you can endure the heat of the situation.

Some people are zealous for God to use them. They dream of doing something significant in their lifetime. All they experience, however, are problems. They blame their lack of success on the problems that they face. If they could realize that those problems are their opportunity to prove themselves, they would rejoice when facing them.

> *Consider it pure joy, my brothers, whenever you face trials of many kinds, because you know that the testing of your faith develops perseverance. Perseverance must finish its work so that you may be mature and complete, not lacking anything.*
>
> James 1:2-4

James is saying that something positive is happening to us during our time of testing. ***Just as a product is never used until it is tested and proven, a person is never used until they are tested and proven.*** So, in the tests that you go through, your capabilities and your potential will be proven. What you can handle, what kind of positions you are suited for in life—these will all be proven in tests. In the following chapters, I am going to share with you nine major tests. These nine are the most common kinds of tests that will be encountered in the life of a Christian.

1

THE TEST OF SMALL THINGS

The Test of Small Things comes to prove our potential for greater opportunities.

Opportunities are usually disguised as hard work, so most people don't recognize them.

—Ann Landers

Be very careful, then, how you live . . . making the most of every opportunity.

Ephesians 5:16A

A Problem, Whether Small or Great, Is Still an Opportunity

The year was 1986. At the age of twenty-six, I had come to the Northwest to build a great church. As I eagerly accepted the opportunity to pastor my first church, I came face to face with Goliath-sized problems.

- An existing mortgage payment that was four thousand dollars more than the church's total monthly income.

- A mountain of debt on accounts payable that had collectors calling and coming to our office demanding payment.
- A remaining congregation of less than one hundred adults that had watched their congregation be separated by strife and decline drastically when their previous pastor resigned.
- A final splitting of the church when I became the pastor. (It's a great morale boost when 20 percent walk out as you walk in!)

My wife, Sheila, was convinced that I was not thinking clearly. Why would I want her and our four-year-old daughter to leave our home, friends and family to move to a little apartment with no furniture? From our home in St. Louis, there was no place we could go in the U.S. and be further away from home. When she asked me for an explanation, I had to be honest with her. My dad, who was my pastor, deserved the same from me.

I could only say to them that I felt strongly that God was asking me to give myself completely to the cause of leading that church into growth and prosperity. There were other men who could, but I was young and unencumbered by other responsibilities at my point of decision. I felt that God was reasoning with me by saying, "See what you can do with this opportunity." I realize this is not what most people say about the call of God, but that was my experience; it was for me a matter of choice. "What would I do with the opportunity?" was the real question.

Fast forward to August 1991. Every goal I had set out to accomplish when I began pastoring, had now been accomplished.

- We were in multiple services on Sunday and had broken the one hundred mark in attendance.
- Our original debt of $1.2 million was cut to less than half.
- We were doing much more than making a mortgage payment: We were supporting a staff with thirty-plus ministries operating in our church.
- Our church was multiplied ten times what it was when we came.

Anyone, who has known a degree of success, knows that success will create problems. Success, in fact, is not a destination but a journey. For those of us in ministry, growth creates the problem of space. Space is necessary, not only to accommodate the ministry, but to continue growing the ministry. We now faced the problem of limited office space, classroom space, nursery space and auditorium space. To solve the space problem, we had to face the "lack of finances" problem. How could we generate the necessary finances to solve the space problem? Anytime you are growing in family, business, or finances, you will continually encounter new problems. The bigger problems you solve, the bigger success you will enjoy.

Fast forward to January 1992. We began to challenge the space problem by receiving our first building fund offering. The next few months were filled with blueprints, engineers and planning meetings. As we faced our need to build, we had decided to look at a five-year plan to accommodate projected growth. While I was preparing to move into a building program, little did I know that God was preparing to offer me another opportunity of a lifetime.

Fast forward to December of 1992. The opportunity had presented itself. We could bypass the five-plus-years building project and move our ministry to the biggest wooden dome in North America. The spacious, state-of-the-art eighty thousand square foot "Peoples Church" had invited me to bring our congregation to their facility. The situation was incredibly familiar to my 1986 opportunity, only of much larger proportions.

- An existing Chapter 11 bankruptcy.
- A long list of accounts payable and unhappy creditors.
- A church congregation weakened and damaged by internal strife and financial struggles.
- A mortgage holder threatening to exercise his options at the end of the Chapter 11 reorganization period.
- The blending of two different congregations who had very different mind-sets.
- The decision of what to do with the duplicate staff members.
- The replacement of the existing mortgage and placement with a new lender.
- Of course, somehow, balance the budget.

Experience Required

I'm convinced that the passing of the previous test had positioned me as a candidate for a greater challenge. Most companies prefer to promote within the organization rather than importing from outside the organization. The method many corporations use is to list job opportunities on bulletin boards or in company papers. Alongside the opportunities, they will list the minimum qualifications. The higher you go in an organization, the more experience is required. Experience is valued above knowledge. You can only learn so much about flying an airplane from a book or classroom. The real test of a pilot is his ability to fly the airplane. In fact, the FAA requires a student pilot to log a minimum amount of flying hours before licensing him as a pilot.

God's kingdom operates in a similar way, with God observing us in real life situations. Many people sit in the classroom every Sunday and read the textbook. God's system for promotion, however, requires the student Christian to log some experience in the application of what they learn in the manual. It's what we do with what we have that proves our potential to handle more. When we are a good student pilot, we qualify to be a copilot, and only when we have done well as a copilot are we a candidate to fly solo. This is a kingdom system of promotion.

You have been faithful with a few things; I will put you in charge of many things.

Matthew 25:21

Back to my new challenge. I knew again that God was saying, "Here's an opportunity. Are you interested?" I'm certain that God would not love me any less if I would have said that I would rather not face those challenges. I'm also certain that I was created for a specific kind of assignment and this new opportunity was tailormade. Mordecai told his niece, Esther:

...who knoweth whether thou art come to the kingdom for such a time as this?

Esther 4:14 (KJV)

What a refreshing thought! **God made me to match the mission.** I'm capable of doing all that God asks me to do. I don't have to do it, but if I choose to, He will empower me to succeed. On January 31, 1993, we had our first service as Covenant Celebration Church—a new church birthed by two congregations, with a vision to take a new territory for the Kingdom of God. Every member of those two churches had to face challenges together, if we were going to succeed. Our theme for our first year was "Whatever It Takes."

- People showed patience with each other, in many cases preferring one another over themselves.
- People gave sacrificially of their finances to our Spring '93 Debt Destruction fund.
- People resisted the predictions of those prophesying our failure.
- One congregation welcomed another to "their house."
- The other congregation came with their families to a whole new environment: One Sunday in one church, the next Sunday in a different one.

By the end of the first year:

- The Chapter 11 was removed.
- The mortgage was placed with a new lender.
- The budget was balanced (as balanced as can be expected for a church who moves by faith!).
- The congregations appeared to have always been together.
- The morale and confidence was high and the people were healthy!

We were promoted! The test was passed, not only by myself, but by the staff, leaders and entire congregation. We were at a new level!

What Are You Doing With What You Have?

When I am considering giving a person an important responsibility in our ministry, I always want to look at how they are handling the responsibilities they already have. Red flags go up if I see:

- A low energy level in approaching their current responsibilities.
- The tendency to be late repeatedly, signaling that their schedule is out of control.
- Their children not getting enough attention at home (this can be observed in the children's behavior).
- Unkempt yard, house or automobile.
- Sloppy appearance or poor hygiene.

Many people see no connection between the kinds of things I'm referencing and how they would handle a more prestigious or public opportunity. *My experience has been that the way a person handles their own personal responsibilities is an accurate indication of how they will handle ministry responsibilities.* One indication to determine whether you are ready for increase, is how well you handle what you have. Some people will read this and quickly respond with, "I'm not doing too bad. I'm doing as well as most people do with what they have." The point I want to make in this chapter is that most people perform in a mediocre way with the opportunities they have in life. What most people do creates the standard we call average. Most average people are offended by the reference to them as being average. However, few decide to actually be above average.

Another common mistake is for a person to conclude that they don't have what it takes to be above average, failing to realize that *it's not what we have that is most important, but it's what we do with what we have.* For example, most people assume that they must be born with a high IQ to excel in life. The truth, however, is that a high IQ can be a liability if it's not balanced by other thinking skills. Some of the most intelligent people in the world work for people of lesser IQs. People of great intelligence are often kept average by poor attitudes, small thinking or "paralysis of analysis." So, being above average in the way you handle life's opportunities, has very little to do with having a high IQ. In fact, brain power itself is included when we say that it's not what you have that's most important, but what you do with what you have.

Can I Handle Increase?

Accurate self-analysis is an important key to increase in our lives. *The people who make the most of life's opportunities are always looking for ways to improve themselves.* These people know it's the little things that most people think don't make any difference, that actually move them beyond mediocrity. Mediocre people even object to and protest when others (usually an employer or teacher) have the "nerve" to say that something minor (being on time, personal appearance, a positive attitude, good family life) has anything to do with them being a responsible person, employee, etc. They defend themselves by saying things like, "I get my job done." This attitude is very common in people who don't realize that some effort, in the areas they consider irrelevant, will actually lift them from being a "C" class person to an "A" class person in their career or ministry. That "A" level is where God finds those who are ready for greater opportunity and can handle increase. If the person is at a "C" level with their current responsibilities, they would be overwhelmed and drop to an "F" (failure) status if given more responsibility. God does not want anyone to fail, thus He provides opportunities within our limitations and ultimately we decide if we can handle increase (not Him).

I can almost hear a defensive person saying, "God doesn't have a class rating, we're all an "A" class to God." Of course we are, when it comes to His love for us. The topic we're discussing is the reward system God has for us. The Bible is clear on the fact that our works are rewarded both now and in eternity, based on what we do with what we have. People who deny this are generally naïve or unproductive and are predicting their lack of productivity. These people want a world system of equality, similar to communism that keeps all men at the same level of increase. Their system denies our God-given potential for ingenuity, creativity and productivity. In that atmosphere, men's dominion nature is harnessed and stifled. Human dignity and morale are destroyed when people have no system of reward for their labors.

Jesus himself told several parables about slothful, unproductive servants. At one point in such a parable, the master ordered that the unproductive servant who had little would lose what he had and that it would be given to a productive servant who already had much (Matthew 25:14-30). God's system of reward is not based on whether someone is a good person at heart. Neither is God's system of increase based on His love for humanity. Rather, both are based on what we do with what we have. This is the ultimate basis on which increase comes to our lives.

The questions below are based on Abraham's increase, and are intended to help you assess your own readiness for increase. Ask yourself the following questions after reading the Scripture reference.

Abram had become very wealthy in livestock and in silver and gold. But the land cold not support them while they stayed together, for their possessions were so great that they were not able to stay together. And quarreling arose between Abram's herdsmen and the herdsmen of Lot.

Genesis 13:2, 6-7

Question: Can I handle increase in my life?

- ◆ Increase means added responsibility—Can I handle it?
- ◆ Increase can cause strife and tension between people— How well do I deal with it?

For example, when you rent a house, you call the landlord. When you own your own house, you are the landlord. When your ministry or business grows, you need more employees to answer the growing number of calls and needs. You may find tension in the changes necessary for staff to best accommodate the increase, because people are generally territorial in nature.

So Abram said to Lot, 'Let's not have any quarreling between you and me, or between your herdsmen and mine, for we are brothers. Is not the whole land before you? Let's part company. If you go to the left, I'll go to the right; if you go to the right, I'll go to the left.'

Genesis 13:8-9

Question: Do I facilitate increase in my life?

- ◆ Do I have the courage to expand beyond where I have become comfortable in my lifestyle?
- ◆ When increase comes, someone must find solutions to the problems that increase causes. Do I know the next needed step to accommodate the increase?

Increase will decrease unless we make room for it. Can you facilitate it or are you frustrated by it? If you are energized by it, you are a candidate for increase. You will find a way, like Abraham, to handle and facilitate the next level in your life, business or ministry.

> *The Lord said to Abram after Lot had parted from him, 'Lift up your eyes from where you are and look north and south, east and west. All the land that you see I will give to you and your offspring forever. Go, walk through the length and breadth of the land, for I am giving it to you.'*
>
> Genesis 13:14-15,17

Question: Do I have a vision for increase?
- Before you will have increase, you have to "see" it. Ask yourself, "Do I see things that are not yet in existence, or can I only see what is a reality today?"
- Are you willing to dream of bigger, better things while not despising the smallness of what you have now? Some people can't do this without feeling discouragement with where they are today.

Notice Abraham had just been trying to accommodate his current increase and God was inviting Him to get vision for future increase. Some would have resisted God's encouragement to "lift up your eyes....walk around in it and imagine increase coming." Some would not have been able to get a vision for increase. How about you? Can you "see" it?

Tips to Help You Pass the Test of Small Things

1. See your problems as opportunities.
Ask yourself, "What's the solution?" Determine what you can do to solve the problem, roll up your sleeves and do it. Don't avoid it; it's your opportunity in work clothes.

2. **Treat small opportunities as if they were your doorway to greater ones.**

Don't despise the responsibilities you have, but be as diligent as you would if the whole world were watching, because God is watching and will promote you when you are proven.

3. **Show motivation in the small things of your everyday life.**

Honest self-analysis should point out areas where you can make a positive difference in yourself as well as your responsibilities. Dig into those areas without procrastination. Abraham Lincoln said, "Prepare yourself and your day will come."

4. **Make no excuses.**

"Excuse-itis" is the disease of non-achievers. People who make excuses never excel with what they have. Give yourself no excuses for doing less than your best with your responsibilities.

2

THE MOTIVATION TEST

The Motivation Test comes upon a person who is doing the right thing, to prove why they are doing what they are doing.

'Does Job fear God for nothing?' Satan replied. 'Have you not put a hedge around him and his household and everything he has? You have blessed the work of his hands, so that his flocks and herds are spread throughout the land. But stretch out your hand and strike everything he has, and he will surely curse you to your face.'

Job 1:9-11

The issue being raised is one of motivation. The accuser of mankind is pressing charges that Job serves God from a wrong motivation. God defends Job, stating that his motives are right. The charges can only be answered one way. Job must prove his potential to serve God in personal crisis and extreme hardship. Unfortunately, Job did not have the privilege of hearing the accusation brought against him and would be tested without knowing it. He could only wonder why this was happening. Such is the nature of The Motivation Test.

Why Do You Do What You Do?

Motive—the compelling force or reason behind a person's actions.

The following questions may appear simple on the surface. In reality, to assure complete accuracy, these questions must be answered in the face of adversity. At a time when every reason to continue is minimal or non-existent, we really discover our true motivation. Since you may not be in a time of testing right now, you should consider these questions as preparation for your eventual time of testing.

1. Why do I go to church?

There are several benefits in belonging to the local church:

- A place to make friends with people who share our faith and values
- The opportunity to use our talents in a corporate setting
- A place for our children to receive Christian education
- Fellowship, activities and sports programs
- A support in times of personal crisis
- A place to have weddings, baby dedications and funerals
- A place to learn Bible principles for life
- A place to be inspired and encouraged

All of these are legitimate benefits in belonging to a church. Sooner or later, however, every Christian will experience a season in their life when these benefits will be withdrawn temporarily. For example, a close church friend may move away. Things are not the same at church anymore. Besides that, some of the people you thought were friends have not been real friendly lately. You may find yourself not wanting to go to church. It's in that setting that our purpose in attending church must be recaptured. The accuser is betting that you will stop attending and drift away from the church. God is hoping you will prove that your motivation is based on more than other people's actions. The right motivation for going to church is one of personal commitment and growth.

> *Let us not give up meeting together, as some are in the habit of doing, but let us encourage one another—and all the more as you see the Day approaching.*
>
> Hebrews 10:25

> *...planted in the house of the Lord, they will flourish in the courts of our God.*
>
> Psalm 92:13

In church, as in any organization where humans are involved, there will always be human errors. As a pastor, I've regretted times when we've overlooked someone or taken a person for granted. Recently at a baby dedication, the secretary left one family off of the list that I use to call the parents forward to dedicate their babies. Fortunately, this couple knew me well enough to know that it was nothing other than human error. Without anyone really noticing, they came forward with everyone else, and we dedicated their baby that day. I could not help but be thankful it had happened to a stable, secure couple. There are people who would have been offended by our mistake. In fact, people leave churches over things like that all the time. When they do so, they miss out on one of God's intentions for putting us together in the first place. God knew we would have personality differences, human errors, disagreements and conflicts.

A major element of our personal development is accomplished by learning how to work through differences, while maintaining a spirit of unity. Our character is strengthened when we get past our fragile feelings, drop our guard and "lock into" the church. Our generation approaches church with a consumer mentality. Unfortunately, this keeps some people "shopping" for a better deal.

Although it's important to consider your needs, when looking for a church home, you must also realize that your relationship with the church is one of giving and receiving. There are seasons when you will be giving more than receiving. You will tend to underestimate the value of the church in your life during that time. But remember, every healthy relationship must have seasons of both giving and receiving. If you left my church today, I would still be preaching next Sunday. You may not show up, but I'll still be doing what God has called me to do. You need to have that same kind of stick-to-it-iveness in your church commitment, so that your motivation can be proven. I am not a pastor so that I can get my back patted. I don't preach on Sunday to hear people say, "Pastor, that was a great message!" When no one compliments me, I don't think to myself, "I've had it with these people. I'm not going to preach again!" You have to be doing ministry for purposes greater than those trivial things.

2. Why do I pray in public?

People who pray or worship in public and fail to do so in private have reason to check their motives.

And when you pray, do not be like the hypocrites, for they love to pray standing in the synagogues and on the street corners to be seen by men. I tell you the truth, they have received their reward in full. But when you pray, go into your room, close the door and pray to your Father, who is unseen. Then your Father, who sees what is done in secret, will reward you.

Matthew 6:5-6

Jesus is not against public worship. He is challenging the Pharisees to stop public worship that is motivated by a desire to impress others. His challenge is to persuade them to worship for the right reason.

Some people falsely judge expression-filled worship as being a show performed for people. However, the Bible teaches congregational praise and worship. The Bible calls us to expression-filled corporate worship.

Praise the Lord. Praise God in His sanctuary; praise Him in His mighty heavens. Praise Him for His acts of power; praise Him for His surpassing greatness. Praise Him with the sounding of the trumpet, praise Him with the harp and lyre, praise Him with tambourine and dancing, praise Him with the strings and flute, praise Him with the clash of cymbals, praise Him with resounding cymbals. Let everything that has breath praise the LORD. Praise the LORD.

Psalm 150

The challenge of public prayer, worship and praise is to do it with the right motives.

3. Why do I give?

In the Old Testament, the Israelites brought the best unspotted lamb that they owned, only to watch it go up in smoke. The next time you give, remember that God wants us to give our best regardless of whether He uses it like we want Him to use it or not. What would you do if next Sunday your pastor said, "Bring your offering so we can burn it"? Most people would say, "No way! I want you to use my money wisely or you won't get any tithe and offering from me."

Although I do agree that we should practice good stewardship with Kingdom finances, the issue we're looking at is one of motivation. We can desire to see ministries be good money managers, but should never make our tithe and offering a conditional practice. You know, the "I'll give if you will do what I want you to do" attitude. I've had several opportunities to receive offerings, with strings attached, that I have not accepted. Generally, if the giver's motivation is right, they will release the control of the offering when they give the offering.

I realize that it's appropriate to designate offerings for a specific cause. There's nothing wrong with that, when offerings are being received for that purpose. However, some people don't give, but rather "exchange" their tithe or offering for a specific thing they desire. In other words, they get something back in exchange for a donation. Tithing and general offerings should be given systematically for your church to use in alignment with the vision of the pastors and leaders. They become responsible before God for stewardship of the tithe and offerings. We receive our blessings, as givers, simply based on our giving and not on ministry stewardship.

The Reason I Do What I Do
Will Ultimately Determine What I Do

Motive is the compelling force behind our actions.

Example #1—People who attend church for the wrong reasons eventually will no longer attend church. I've watched men come to church to make a girlfriend happy. Eventually, unless they find a right reason for attending, they stop coming. The motivation for attending church is tested when they get married or break off the relationship. He was attending church for her, when it was required to be a candidate for marriage. Now that he's married her, the original motivation does not exist. So, the real reason for going will now determine what he will do. In this case, without a new reason for going, he is no longer motivated to attend.

Example #2—People who get married for the wrong reasons must find a right reason for staying together if they expect it to last a lifetime. An unexpected pregnancy has caused many couples to feel as if they had to get married. Two wrongs don't make a right. Other individuals get married for fear they may not get another chance. Temporary reasons, motivating these kind of marriages today, will not continue to motivate the marriage forever. Ultimately, if these people do not find a right basis for their marriage, they end up confessing to each other, counselors and ministers why they married in the first place. If you listen to them, the amazing thing is that often the original reason they got married is now the reason for divorce! They say, "I only married because I was pregnant," or "I felt pressure to marry." **Remember this: the reason I do what I do will ultimately determine what I do.**

Motivation Is a Matter of the Heart

Lasting motivation proceeds forth from the heart. People can be temporarily motivated by other people and things around them. Permanent, enduring motivation, however, can only come from within.

> *Above all else, guard your heart, for it is the wellspring of life.*
>
> Proverbs 4:23

The wellspring of life! In other words, the place from which our behavior and lifestyle is motivated. The source of our words and actions is our heart. The Bible pinpoints two ways that the content of our heart is revealed.

1. The words of our mouth.

You brood of vipers, how can you who are evil say anything good? For out of the overflow of the heart the mouth speaks.
                                                                Matthew 12:34

When you are not on guard, the nature of your words will reveal the content of your heart. Those "private" conversations or slips of the tongue reveal:

- the critic in you
- the fantasies in you
- the anger in you
- the hurt in you

These are an indication of why you do what you do. When you see the content of your heart, you can know what is motivating you to do what you do. Many people today speak out of hurt that has not been healed. That hurt from a past relationship or bad experience is a motivating force in their life. By hearing them talk, you get an indication of why they don't trust others. Their motivation is unhealthy and will unfortunately hinder positive relationships in their future.

2. The way we spend our money.

For where your treasure is, there your heart will be also.
                                                                Matthew 6:21

I haven't spent any money on mountain climbing equipment, parachuting, motorcycle riding or snow skiing. While I have friends who invest their money in all of these, I wouldn't buy a parachute at 90 percent off the sale price. I don't have any desire to jump out of an airplane! I have, on the other hand, invested in some golf clubs and racquet-ball equipment. What motivates me to reach in my wallet may be different than what motivates you. However, something motivates all of us. When it comes to the way we spend our money, the most powerful motivation comes from within. To know the motivations of your heart, simply look at where your "treasures" are going. Your treasures and your heart are in the same place.

There are other indicators of motivation, but one thing is sure—motivation is a matter of the heart. Because men are only able to see each other outwardly, it's easy to pass wrong judgment on other people. God, on the other hand, sees the heart.

> But the LORD said to Samuel, 'Do not consider his appearance or his height, for I have rejected him. The LORD does not look at the things man looks at. Man looks at the outward appearance, but the LORD looks at the heart.'
>
> I Samuel 16:7

We're Not Stuck with Wrong Motives

One of the most common errors people make is to think that they are stuck with whatever is in their heart. When a person feels victimized by wrong motives, they will say, "I can't help it, that's just me. It will never change." I have good news for you. You can change the content of your heart! You and I have the ability to take out what we want to get rid of and replace it with what we desire to have in our heart.

For most people, the garage in their house is the place where stuff piles up. Old stuff, stuff we don't know what to do with, stuff we're not even sure how we got. We all know that, if we just let it happen, we can accumulate all kinds of unwanted junk in the garage. Think of your heart as a garage. You may have some stuff you are emotionally attached to, but it's junk. You would be better off without it. There's old stuff from previous generations. They dumped it on you and you continue to let it happen. There's stuff that so-called friends left you holding for them. You feel obligated to hold on to it. It's not your stuff, but they are your friends, so now you've accumulated some more extra baggage inside of you.

Approach your heart with a sense of ownership and responsibility. Ask God to help you cleanse yourself of wrong motives and replace them with right ones. There's a right reason for doing every right thing we do. We must assume responsibility for maintaining those good and proper motives. Don't stop doing a good thing if your reason for doing it is wrong. Rather, change your reason for doing it. You're not stuck with wrong motives.

Pay Attention to Those Things You Want to Have in Your Heart

My son, pay attention to what I say; listen closely to my words. Do not let them out of your sight, keep them within your heart; for they are life to those who find them and health to a man's whole body. Above all else, guard your heart, for it is the wellspring of life.

Proverbs 4:20-23

The eyes and the ears are windows into the heart. What you continually focus your attention on will enter your heart. As the content of your heart changes, your motives will change. All of us have suffered an injustice from another person. When the incident occurs, we may find ourselves lying awake at night imagining how we will get revenge. Our mind races to visualize the "dirty, rotten scoundrel" getting what they deserve. At this stage, our attention is on the injustice and thus our motivation is to get even. Hopefully, our attention doesn't stay there. Hopefully, we purpose to shake it off and not dwell on it. As we move our attention to other things, our motivation to "even the score" will change.

After enough time passes, with little or no attention on the injustice, we may experience other motivations as we reflect back on the incident. Now we may be motivated to forgive them or have compassion on them, rather than being motivated to strangle them. How did this change? The motivation changed when we changed the focus of our attention from getting revenge to getting over it. We can choose what takes up residence in our heart, by choosing where we focus our attention.

My Harvest Is in My Heart

Consider this statement:
The single most important element in a person's future is the content of his heart.

> *Make a tree good and its fruit will be good, or make a tree bad and its fruit will be bad, for a tree is recognized by its fruit....The good man brings good things out of the good stored up in him, and the evil man brings evil things out of the evil stored up in him.*
>
> Matthew 12:33, 35

To understand this Scripture, we must realize the meaning of the terms *fruit* and *tree*.

Fruit represents the ways of a person's life. It includes habits, behavior, conversation, relationships, success or failures.

Tree represents the person's heart. It encompasses thoughts, attitudes, emotions and will.

Jesus is teaching here that people are like trees, in that we produce on the outside, based on what is on the inside. Just like healthy fruit is a sign of a healthy tree, likewise, good things in a man's life are a sign of good things in a man's heart. In Washington State, we are proud of our apples. We have the world's best apples (to fully believe that, it helps to be from Washington).

Imagine a farmer who has an apple orchard and is disappointed in the quality of the apples. They are infected, ugly and no good. So what does he do? Would he say, "The barn is the problem. I need to paint the barn red so I can grow healthy apples"? Would he say, "It's the pickup truck I'm driving. If I get a new model, I'll grow better apples"? You and I both know the farmer would not react to a bad harvest of apples by painting the barn or buying a new truck. Yet, that's how a lot of people respond to the bad harvest of their lives. They place responsibility and blame for their problems on everything except the tree that produced the fruit! They blame other people, they blame the government, they go get a new wife or move to a different church. When a person doesn't deal with the unhealthy tree, the harvest won't change regardless of how many other changes they make. The harvest is a result of the heart.

Games People Play

Game playing is a favorite pastime in our society. It matches the wit, intelligence, courage, strength and endurance of people.

In fact, we like games so much we spend millions on stadiums, arenas, television air time, skilled players and athletes so we can have games. We have game shows, games stores, games based on games…we are into playing games.

Game playing can be fun, challenging and harmless when on a playing field or a game board. However, when the mentality of a game spills over into life, it can damage family, career, reputation, health and relationship with God. There are three reasons people drift into game playing on the field of life.

1. People play games to avoid facing reality.

People play emotional and mental games to avoid facing an unwanted reality. This game is most commonly called "denial." The basic strategy is, "If I ignore the problem and pretend it doesn't exist, it will go away." Recently, someone mentioned to me that the tire on my Jeep looked flat. Now, I could have pretended that it wasn't, but that wouldn't have changed anything. When I got up the next day, the tire would still be flat.

Don't consider the recognition of your flat tire as compounding the problem. You already have a problem and recognizing it is the first step toward a solution. In my situation, I was able to do some temporary fixing by putting air in the tire and delaying the actual repair. This is possible and sometimes appropriate with situations in life. In the meantime, I was looking at my calendar and planning the best time to fix my tire. I was delaying the confrontation, but not ignoring it. Make sure your delays are not a denial, because the tire will not get fixed on its own.

2. People play games to make themselves appear different than they are.

A person is in danger of complete failure when it becomes more important to keep a secret than to solve a problem. For example, many men today find it difficult to receive counsel for their marriage. The male ego struggles with letting anyone know that he needs help. Unfortunately, many troubled relationships never improve because secret keeping is the primary motivation rather than problem solving. "Keeping up the image" has been the downfall of many businesses, churches and homes.

3. People play games to avoid participation.

Many of the games people play are learned early in life. A ten year old can't tell his parents "Look, I don't want to go to school today, I'm tired and want the day off." So, since that won't get him anywhere, he must put on his "sick" face and "sick" voice and murmur, "I don't feel good today." If executed well, this kind of acting could get him out of going to school. In this same way adults play games to avoid going to the in-laws' house, Junior's ball game, or another undesirable event. Oftentimes, just pretending you don't see someone can get you out of having to speak to them.

When a person's actions are motivated by these shallow, philosophical games, life will be fragile at best. Authenticity and a commitment to enduring principles are the highest level of motivation. These alone guarantee real, genuine, Godly and lasting success.

3

The Credibility Test

**This test comes to prove our
reliability and trustworthiness.**

*...Well done...You have been faithful with a few things;
I will put you in charge of many things.*

Matthew 25:23

The gaining and maintaining of credibility is what opens the door of your next opportunity. For example, if a person is interested in being hired for a specific career position, they must first establish credibility with the person who is doing the hiring. The Credibility Test will question various aspects in a person's life as they pertain to the opportunity before them. Passing the test will mean a promotion into the new career. When you stop and consider this, you can't help but realize that most, if not all, of life's promotions occur based on passing some form of credibility test.

Credibility is a compilation of :

1. What I do
2. Who I am, and
3. How others view me

When someone has a credibility problem, it may have more to do with perception than with facts. In today's high-tech media form of communication, perception can be far from reality. This is why public personalities often experience a credibility gap between them and the person the public sees them as being. Closing the gap is essential to maintaining public credibility. Part of growing and increasing in life is to grow and increase in favor with God and man.

And Jesus grew in wisdom and stature, and in favor with God and men.
                                                          Luke 2:52

Recently, I was approached by an individual who wanted to know how to become a teacher. This man regarded himself as being gifted to teach and had the desire to teach. As he spoke to me, he shared this desire hoping that I could tell him what to do. Similar questions are common to men and women who are hoping to get a shot at public ministry. Not unlike athletes, actors and musicians around the world who are waiting to be discovered, these sincere people await an opportunity. What is difficult for these desiring people to understand is that we are not something until others regard us as such. Therefore, we must all seek credibility with others.

For example, a man claiming to be a tailor can go to tailor school, open a tailor shop and hang out a sign that identifies him as a tailor. The real proof, however, that he is indeed a tailor is when he has customers. In fact, without customers, eventually the sign will come down and the shop will close. There will be no tailor shop and there will be no tailor. The hope for the "wanna-be" tailor is to establish credibility, not only as a tailor but as an exceptional one. That credibility is essential in the proving of his potential.

No One Else Can Earn Your Credibility

To further the example of a tailor, let's imagine that the tailor shop is now established and the tailor has a great reputation. One evening a stranger walks into the shop and asks if he could be allowed to do some tailoring of his own in the tailor's shop. "In fact," he says, "would it be possible for me to begin tomorrow morning?" All of the credibility earned by the tailor's shop is insufficient to make this newcomer a tailor. He will only be a tailor if others regard him as being one (including the owner of the shop). The credibility cannot be given, it must be earned. The newcomer may first only have to earn it with the owner, but eventually his credibility will have to extend beyond that, if he is going to be a tailor. You see, we can all receive mentoring from others. All of us can learn from others. But eventually each of us will pass or fail our own credibility test.

There are three forms of credibility that contribute to the proving of your personal potential. They are:

1. The credibility of competence
2. The credibility of personality
3. The credibility of character

Let's take a more in-depth look at all three.

Once people know that you know what you're doing, they will find it easier to work with you. This credibility is earned when you:

- *are proven to have the necessary skills for the role you are in.* Communication, organization, technical, and leadership, etc.
- *are proven to have the knowledge necessary for the role you are in.* Education, experience or natural instinct may all contribute to earning the credibility of competence.
- *are proven to have the right kind of habits for the role you are in.* For example, some people are required to stay in good physical condition and mental alertness to be competent for their job. Police officers, airline pilots and air traffic controllers are required to maintain habits of discipline. A variance from this will endanger their credibility for competence.

One of the things God wants to know, before He places you, is that you can do the job. God doesn't set men up for failure. Men may set themselves up to fail, but God will not give us more responsibility than we can handle. This is why men should not force doors open in their own lives, but rather wait on God's timing. You may know where you are going in life, but if you attempt to go ahead of schedule, you will find yourself incompetent and suffering the loss of credibility.

The equipping of oneself, so that you remain competent, is an ongoing, never ending task. What may have been considered fresh and cutting edge just five years ago, may now be outdated and inefficient. Methods and skills are constantly being improved in every area of life. Yesterday's success may be applauded, respected or honored, but the credibility of competence is a credibility based on what I can do today. This credibility is earned by performance, not by respect, love, honesty, courage or other important virtues.

For example, some people expect this kind of credibility to be automatically extended to them on the basis of friendship. They reason that friends who have hiring power should hire friends who are unemployed on the basis of friends helping friends. This kind of reasoning overlooks the importance of competence as well as other kinds of credibility. It does not reflect on a father's love for his ten year old son, when he denies him the opportunity to drive the car. It may appear to the child that, "If Dad really loved me, he would let me drive the car."

Reality, however, is that Dad can still love his son very much and judge him as being untrained, unskilled, or not ready and presently incompetent to drive the car. *It's not a question of love, it's a question of competence.* We have to remember this in the big people's world as well. Whatever we strive for or attempt to achieve in life can only happen by earning the credibility of competence.

- Do you want to build houses?
- Do you want to do people's taxes?
- Do you want to be an educator?
- Do you want to practice law?
- Do you want to make food people will love to eat?
- Do you want to fly airplanes?
- Do you want to be a counselor?
- Do you want to lead a Bible study?

Doing whatever it is you want to do, involves earning the credibility of competence.

You will often hear people comment, after meeting a famous person, "She is a really nice person," or "I can't believe how down-to-earth he was." These encounters can make a permanent impression on all of us, either positive or negative. This credibility is not based on talent, skill or character. It's established rather on a person's traits. Politicians win thousands, even millions of votes on the credibility of personality. This credibility is one that we may not want to give much regard to, especially by itself. However, a pleasing personality is a tremendous aid in establishing our credibility with other people. Those who pass it off as unimportant, will limit their own potential in life. Those who consider it to be the only form of credibility that is important, will eventually suffer the loss of life's gains. This credibility is earned by:

- *having a positive effect on others when they are in our presence.* They feel our attitude and it feels good.
- *practicing common courtesies toward others.* A smile, good manners, genuine concern for them, hospitality, openness, etc.

Many people are hindered in life by an unpleasant personality. They may have a servant's heart and great intentions, but their personality is *"blah."* People are uncomfortable around them and may even avoid being with them. In ministry, I've seen individuals who didn't realize what happened when they joined a ministry team and soon became the team! Everyone else was repelled by this one individual's personality. If a person is blind to this, they go through life repelling people and never knowing why. Negativity is the chief cause for a person having an unpleasant personality.

A negative personality will bring heaviness to a light and enjoyable conversation. A negative personality sees only problems and not solutions. Since everyone has his own share of challenges, people consciously or subconsciously avoid exposure to additional negativity in their lives. The way we identify and avoid people who have a negative personality provides the basis for the loss of their personality credibility. Listed below are six questions to ask yourself to help you recognize negativity in your own life.

A Checkup from the Neck Up

1. What do I think about most?
- Thoughts that trouble me or make me irritable?
- Thoughts that encourage me and make me feel confident?

2. How do I respond to problems or difficulties?
- Am I challenged or discouraged?
- Do I solve or do I compound problems?

3. What do I do when I hear negative feedback?
- A negative person quickly attaches negative feedback to their self-worth and becomes defensive. The positive person can separate the feedback from their self-worth, making them more objective and able to improve.

4. How comfortable am I with failure or defeat?
- Positive people have glitches, mistakes or setbacks, but not failures or defeat. Negative people, on the other hand, expect failure and they get it.

5. What kind of people do I get along well with?
- Anyone? What are they like (be honest)? Are they confident, encouraging, successful?

6. How do I respond to positive information?
- Do books, literature, speeches tend to inspire and motivate me?
- Am I critical of people who have experienced success?
- Do I accept the value of faith and confidence for my life or do I disregard it as shallow and unimportant?

Negative people always pride themselves in being more of a realist that the positive people around them. A negative person usually fails to recognize the difference in noticing the negative and being negative. A positive personality can be aware that the economy is slumping without having to elaborate on it or get depressed by it. A negative personality, however, will make it the headline of his day and offer no encouragement to those around him.

When the disease of negativity grows within a person, he himself will deny reality. A negative personality is blind to life's blessings and God's promises. A negative personality has a different reality than a positive personality. Neither reality is more realistic than the other. They are both very real to the individual and to life. Life has pain, hardship and problems. Life also has joy, pleasure and blessings. To have a positive personality, one does not have to deny life's realities but simply focus on the good.

Finally, brothers, whatever is true, whatever is noble, whatever is right, whatever is pure, whatever is lovely, whatever is admirable—if anything is excellent or praiseworthy—think about such things.
Philippians 4:8

Some other tips for earning the credibility of personality that you can continually strive to do are:

- Manage your moods
- Smile often with your face and your voice
- Greet others without waiting for them to greet you first
- See the people around you as having high value
- Speak fluently, words of blessing and inspiration to others
- Practice motivational maintenance of your own life (get plenty of rest, exercise and faith food)

Recently, I was speaking in a Sunday morning service, when I said, "If your employer is demanding that you do something that violates your conscience, go in tomorrow and quit your job." John Holloway II was in the audience that day. Believing that was a direct word for him, he quit work on Monday. The following is a letter he wrote me:

Dear Pastor,

Three Sundays ago, March 12th, my wife and I visited Covenant Celebration Church for the very first time. After you had given your message you spoke out a word, that if anyone was in a job in which it caused them to lie, they needed to quit immediately. Specifically to go in and resign on Monday morning. Well, that word was for me! In the last six months, I have been struggling over the lying it took for me to sometimes sell advertising for my company. Primarily, because I did not believe in the program at all. Being afraid to quit, with only $200 in my account, a wife and two kids to support, I went and quit my job on Monday. Immediately, I went to look for a new job. The first week I applied for 14 jobs and had seven interviews. All I got was four hours work in a warehouse with a temp job company. But that earned us enough money to keep going on for the next week.

Week two, I put in seven resumes and had three interviews, and worked one day in a sausage factory for this temp job company. That again earned us enough money to keep going on for the next week.

The following Wednesday, March 29th, I landed a new job. Not any job, but one that was beyond what I could have hoped for. Instead of straight commission, I received a salary plus. Also, medical benefits, retirement and projected earnings of almost twice the amount I was previously earning. Plus, a nice trip to Florida for training as well!

I just wanted to let you know, because I thought God should get all the glory, for He is faithful to His Word.

There were two obvious tests in this experience. First, there was the authority test (discussed in the previous chapter); second, there was the credibility of character test. John made a decision to withdraw from the authority that was placing him in a position that compromised his character. In making this decision, John was passing the test and promotion was sure to follow. The promotion did not come immediately, but John maintained character in a difficult circumstance. This is where some people lose their reward—by becoming impatient and breaking character.

Stay in Character

Our church in Tacoma, Washington is the producer of one of the nation's largest outdoor passion plays. Nearly forty thousand people come every summer to our amphitheater to experience "the greatest story ever told." For actors and actresses, there is still nothing more challenging than a live stage performance. On television you can cut, paste, edit and shoot again until you get a scene perfect. In live theater, however, the show must go on!

We have had actors forget lines, come on stage for their scene, trip and fall down at exactly the wrong moment. Technicians have forgotten to turn on a soundtrack; horses have backed our chariots into the water, bucked the riders off and lifted their tails for a manure deposit on the set at the worst possible time in the play. Camels have laid down in the dirt street to "waller," and sheep have run out of the amphitheater and into the parking lot. With fourteen years of performances, we've seen our share of unexpected, unplanned occurrences that have the potential to distract an audience. Good actors, however, know one important response to the undesirable interruption: *stay in character!* It's the rule of the live stage. It's the ability to stay on course and continue with the scene as if nothing happened. The predetermined character, being played by an actor, cannot be compromised regardless of what happens around him. The sign of a good actor is to not break character in difficult situations.

Likewise, our character ethics are never known until they are tested. We may have good intentions, but intentions are not the same as good characters. ***Good character is the moral strength to maintain our preplanned course of good intentions in the moment of opposition.*** At that specific moment, it is tempting to break character. The circumstances seem to justify it. The weak will break and compromise. Only the strong survive. The difference in maintaining stage character and moral character is that moral character is often challenged in private, while stage character is challenged in public. Perhaps the greatest opponent to moral and ethical character is the voice that whispers, "Nobody will ever know, so what can it hurt?" It's in that moment of potential compromise, that one must be true to himself. When we are true to ourselves, we pass the greatest character test of all. It's only then, when we are honest with ourselves, that we are prepared to be honest with God and other people.

Truth Within

When a prophet named Nathan confronted David with his sin (2 Samuel 12), he first had to awaken him from an obvious state of denial. David, who was a man after God's own heart, had apparently justified his sin of adultery with Bathsheba in his own mind. It appears that he was moving on with his life as if nothing had happened. "De-nial," contrary to what many people believe, is not a river in Egypt. Denial is the blocking out of truth in the inner man.

Someone who is in denial does not know that they are; they genuinely fail to acknowledge an obvious reality. This person has a "blind spot" which is hindering their perspective. Nathan's approach to David was to tell him a parable about a rich man, who though he had much, took the only small lamb that a poor man had. David, who was king, thought that Nathan was referring to a real incident within his kingdom and demanded to know who had done such a terrible thing. While David's mind was open to injustice, Nathan rifled back the answer, "David, you are the man!" Imagine how David felt at that instant. Like taking a powerful slap on the face, he is shocked by this confrontation. It was in this moment, when truth was unveiled, that David's future would be decided.

The pride of life is the cover-up most people use when their own character credibility is at stake. Those who choose this cover-up, go back into denial. Fortunately, David did not choose to cover up his moral failure. He did not become defensive and guarded. He welcomed truth and allowed her voice to speak. He listened with his heart to the evidence she presented him that day. When she had taken him back in his memory and revealed to him his wrongs, truth rested her case and

David repented. This was a great day in the life of David. Rather than losing credibility, he gained it. His ability to be honest with himself was a sign of great character.

The blind spot was torn away and David was seeing clearly again. It was then, in the midst of his own failure, that David did not make excuses. He did not blame others. He chose to be authentic and honest. This level of self-honesty enabled him to then be honest with God. Psalm 51 records that prayer. Notice his understanding of his own need for inner truth.

Have mercy on me, O God, according to your unfailing love; according to your great compassion, blot out my transgressions.

Surely you desire truth in the inner parts; you teach me wisdom in the inmost place. Cleanse me with hyssop, and I will be clean; wash me, and I will be whiter than snow.

Create in me a pure heart, O God, and renew a steadfast spirit within me. Do not cast me from your presence or take your Holy Spirit from me. Restore to me the joy of your salvation and grant me a willing spirit, to sustain me.

Psalm 51:1, 6-7, 10-12

Inside-Out Living

Recently I was on a Christian TV program in which the host appeared to struggle with the idea of Christians wanting to succeed in life. I don't understand this struggle, when God Himself has given us formulas for success.

*Do not let this Book of the Law depart from your mouth;
meditate on it day and night, so that you may be careful
to do everything written in it. Then you will be prosperous and successful.*

Joshua 1:8

My host proceeded to ask the question, "What's
the difference in the world's approach to success and the
message we are hearing from authors and speakers like
yourself?" "It's very simple," I said, "the world approaches success from the outside in, while God's approach is
from the inside out." My example of John Holloway II
refusing to compromise his character to keep his job, is a
prime example of "inside-out" living. The worldly
approach would have been to place higher value on keeping the job than on telling the truth. This inverted
approach to success creates an environment for eventual
failure. God's plan for success (inside out) is consistently
drawing our attention to our own character. By focusing
on the ethics of our heart, we can be assured that good
things will come out of our lives.

*The good man brings good things out of the good stored
up in him...*

Matthew 12:35

Credibility Leads to Influence

When a person passes The Credibility Test, they
enlarge their sphere of influence. People only allow others to
influence them to the degree that those others have earned
credibility with them. As Christians, it's important that we
increase our influence in society. The only way this will happen is by an increase of credibility in Christians.

The world has seen the "dirty laundry" of Christian leaders and all of us have dealt with a loss of credibility. Society doesn't understand God's grace and gift of righteousness like we do. Society only understands credibility or lack of it. God may never have people who are perfect, but He is going to have people who will pass The Credibility Test and have growing influence on our world. We gain this credibility...

* As we become equipped with the thoughts and ways of God
* As we live with faith-filled minds, hearts, and faces
* As we show integrity and ethics in our relationships
* As we model parenthood, training our children
* As we build strong marriages
* As we succeed in our chosen careers and vocations
* As we help people who are hurting and begin to heal our world
* As we prosper and manage our finances well

These very real accomplishments, in the lives of Christians, will give credibility and increase our influence in the earth. The valuable result is that men will honor and glorify our Father in heaven. Let's pass this test!

...that they may see your good deeds and praise your Father in heaven.

Matthew 5:16

4

THE WILDERNESS TEST

The Wilderness Test comes in the form of a drought or dry season. This test will prove your potential to make the changes necessary to enter the next level of prosperity in your life.

He led you through the vast and dreadful desert, that thirsty and waterless land with its venomous snakes and scorpions. He brought you water out of hard rock. He gave you manna to eat in the desert, something your father had never known, to humble and to test you so that in the end it might go well with you.

Deuteronomy 8:15-16

While en route to possessing their promised land, the people had to pass through the wilderness. The wilderness was a necessary part of the journey. It was between them and their destination. Likewise, our course will include some "dry" places. There will be times when questions are many and answers are few and times when God's "felt" presence seems so far away. You survive, but you don't thrive here. The blessings of abundance are beyond this place. Your supply does not match your demand. *Don't get used to it …God doesn't want you to take* *up residence there.* He doesn't want you to live there. He wants you to overcome and move on to better things.

The Right Response to the Wilderness

Your response to the wilderness will determine how long you stay in the wilderness. Unfortunately, the perils of the wilderness can cause a person to become disoriented and confused. The result is that people get stuck in this dry, desertlike place and end up going around in circles, struggling to reach their destiny. To pass the test of the wilderness, a person must respond properly to the perils of the wilderness. The wrong response holds you in the dry place, while a proper response provides the passage out. Let's identify three important responses that will help you pass through the wilderness in the shortest possible time.

1. Keep an attitude of gratitude

Don't complain about what you don't have, but focus on what you do have. The wilderness has a way of distorting the facts and showing you an inaccurate perspective of things. Even in dry times there are plenty of things to be thankful for. Maintain your attitude of gratitude.

> *...give thanks in all circumstances, for this is God's will for you in Christ Jesus.*
> 1 Thessalonians 5:18

2. Don't fix the blame, fix the problem

So many people fall into the "blame game." They are suffering hardship, so they blame their parents, boss, government, neighbor or whoever they can. Even if someone contributed to your burden, don't waste your energy on placing blame. Put your energy into fixing the problem.

3. Don't look back

Life has no rewind button. To replay yesterday is to lose today. Reflecting on the "good old days" has caused many to miss out on today's possibilities.

Do not say, 'Why were the old days better than these?'
For it is not wise to ask such questions.
Ecclesiastes 7:10

Conquering Containment

To contain is to "hold back or restrain within fixed limits." The strategy of evil is to contain good in order to:

- Keep people from growing and prospering
- Keep every good work from increasing

If you dream of improving your lifestyle or improving the world, you've entered a battle against containment. Three areas we must constantly oppose containment in are:

1. Our lifestyle
2. Our community
3. Our church

I'm told that if you put fleas in a jar with a lid on it, they jump up repeatedly and hit their heads on the lid, trying to get out. After repeated bumps on the head, however, they learn their limitations. Now you can take the lid off and they will stay in the jar. They remain there completely unaware of the "air up there." Likewise, the "lid" of the wilderness has a way of conditioning us to stay within fixed boundaries. Too many bumps from past experiences cause us to lose our enthusiasm for life. We don't realize that the lid was only temporary. The lid was only there for a season. Now the lid is off, and God has great possibilities for us. Perhaps containment is holding you in old patterns that have no risk of pain.

In Genesis 30 is the story of two men named Laban and Jacob. Jacob worked hard and wanted to prosper. Laban did everything he could to contain Jacob and see his dreams denied. There are two powerful messages in this story:

1. Delayed is not denied

Just because your dream of better things has not happened yet, don't give up. A dream delayed is not necessarily a dream denied. Jacob thought it would happen sooner, but he stayed on course pursuing his dream for twenty years. Eventually, everything he had worked for was achieved.

2. Man cannot stop God's blessing

Although Laban cheated him and changed his wages ten times, Jacob's hard work and perseverance brought him great wealth and blessings. Be encouraged by this story. *Man cannot stop God's blessing from coming into your life.* When we do the things required to prosper, by God's principles, nothing can hinder our eventual blessing.

Avoiding the Wilderness Routine

One strong characteristic of the wilderness is that of a routine lifestyle. Remember, the object is to pass the test and move on. The wilderness is not where you want to stay. *The problem with tolerating, is that it leads to acceptance.* Once we have tolerated wilderness ways long enough, it gets easier to accept them as a permanent way of life. We accept that it will never get better. By accepting it, we then establish it. Many people have fallen into routine marriage habits. Others have become what I call "routine Christians."

It's easy for routine to take over in the wilderness, causing us to enter a cycle of repetitive action that is getting us nowhere new. Not much changes and nothing gets better in the routine mode. Routine Christianity is a lifestyle of Christian practice that is lacking Christian progress or vision. This condition is marked by an increasing void of joy and satisfaction. Complaining becomes normal everyday conversation when a person is in the cycle of routine Christianity.

SEVEN SYMPTOMS OF ROUTINE CHRISTIANITY

R = Rut of repeated, boring, and unrewarding activity.

O = Obstinate state of mind which causes a person to resist change by being stubborn and inflexible.

U = Unbelief that hinders a person from entering into greater things for their life.

T = Traditions involving methodology, that no longer best serve their original purpose, but continue to own our allegiance.

I = Ignorance resulting from failure to gain knowledge and understanding.

N = The nature of the flesh being allowed to fulfill its desires that are contrary to God's Word.

E = An empty spirit that is desertlike and lacks the resources to provide life and vitality.

The Great Adventure

Life was not meant to be routine. Life was meant to be progressive, new and adventurous.

I have come that they may have life, and have it to the full.
John 10:10

Steven Curtis Chapman sings a song that has inspired me with courage through the changes in my life. The song is entitled "The Great Adventure." Look closely at the words of the chorus:

Saddle up your horses
We've got a trail to blaze
Through the wild blue yonder
Of God's amazing grace
Let's follow our leader
Into the glorious unknown
This is life like no other
This is the great adventure!

Breaking Out—Breaking In

Breaking out of the wilderness can cause you to break in to a new level of abundance. The wilderness cannot hold you after you make the proper adjustments. David looked back at the testing of his ancestors and rejoiced at the final outcome of abundance.

For you, O God, tested us; you refined us like silver. You brought us into prison and laid burdens on our backs. You let men ride over our heads; we went through fire and water, but you brought us to a place of abundance.
Psalm 66:10-12

In a similar way, the test of the wilderness is designed for a better end, not a bitter one. What is it we need to break out of?

Let's revisit again the seven symptoms of routine Christianity, with a *"break out"* in mind.

The Rut

When was the last time you did something for the first time? Many people today live in the city of Boredomville as if it's the only place on Earth. Boring people live in Boredomville. They have boring jobs, boring homes, boring marriages and they attend boring churches. The truth, however, is that it's not the job, home, marriage or church—it's the person who is boring. If your life is boring, talk to the person in the mirror tomorrow morning and tell them to "get a life." Decide today to leave the rut of Boredomville.

Likewise, don't confuse activity with accomplishment. Just because the wheels are spinning and some mud is flying, doesn't mean you're going somewhere. Unless you're moving, the scenery stays the same and that scenery is less than exciting. Accomplishment, on the other hand, will bring forward motion and the discovery of new territory. Even being busy can be boring unless you're making progress.

Obstinate State of Mind

The place of promise is just beyond your wilderness experience. Don't get stuck in a state of mind that resists changes in yourself. Keep expecting to learn and grow yourself into the next level. There are attitudes to adjust, like sails adjust to winds, which will move you forward to new things.

Unbelief

Recently I went for a physical exam. The doctors hooked me up to a monitor and put me on a treadmill. They continued to increase the speed, pushing me to my maximum potential. They were testing the strength of my heart. The only way to know the heart's strength is to put it under pressure and watch how it performs. Faith is not known until it is tested by difficult circumstances. The wilderness reveals unbelief, as you stop anticipating God's fulfillment of His promises. Unbelief keeps people in routine and out of the promised land.

Tradition

Tradition has held people in dry places. It causes misplaced loyalty, resulting in an obligation and allegiance to the wrong people or things. Tradition can be good when it is providing progress and growth. When it begins to hinder our journey toward our promised land, it must be evaluated. Be quick to change unproductive methods and locate a new and productive one.

For Christian leaders, it's important to not confuse methods with the message. *The message is sacred; methods are not.* The Gospel message will adapt well to different cultures. The Gospel message can be packaged for different age groups and ethnic diversity. Some people struggle with different music styles and presentations of the Gospel. These things are only methods and should change and adapt to various people groups. These methods should change with the surroundings in order to relate to people. So, keep your allegiance to the spreading of the Gospel message and avoid getting "hung up" or stuck into a tradition involving methods.

Ignorance

The routine may continue until your knowledge increases enough to take you into a new place. People often say "the truth will set you free" thinking that they are quoting Scripture. In actuality, that quotation is incomplete. The Scripture in its entirety says, "You shall know the truth and the truth will set you free" (John 8:32). It's not the *presence* of truth that will deliver you from the wilderness, but the *knowledge* of truth. Say to yourself, "The truth cannot help me, unless I know it." As you say this, you're beginning to realize how ignorance can stop you and hold you in an unwanted routine.

> *...my people are destroyed from lack of knowledge.*
> Hosea 4:6

- Knowledge is the gathering of information
- Understanding is the interpretation of information
- Wisdom is the application of information

The Nature of the Flesh

Grumbling, complaining and accusing were all hindering the dream of the promised land from becoming reality. What about you? What one thing are you doing that is hindering your progress? You may have thought of it as family tradition and accepted it as a harmless mannerism. If it's not hindering you, it's not harmless.

> *Dear friends, I urge you, as aliens and strangers in the world, to abstain from sinful desires, which war against your soul.*
> 1 Peter 2:11

Begin now to ask God to help you break the gravity-like pull of unwanted negative habits that hold you back from your full potential. The ways of the flesh war against the wellness of your soul.

Emptiness of Spirit

Just as the desert lacks the resources to provide life and vitality, a dry spirit lacks the ability to provide those things that bring personal growth. Your spirit holds the fuel of life and when it's empty, you find yourself in a drained, weary condition. A lack of inspiration will make it impossible to journey on to your destination. You can keep the life of God flowing into your spirit with singing, praising, reading, hearing and proclaiming God's Word in your life. Three habits for spiritual health are found in Ephesians 5:18:

1. *I should speak to others in psalms, hymns and spiritual songs.* This can only happen in church services, prayer meetings and places where believers impact faith to one another through our words and songs.
2. *I should sing and make music in my heart.* Notice the encouragement to make the music. Create a song within.
3. *I should always give thanks to God for everything.* When we express appreciation for life's blessings, our spirits are refreshed and lifted.

Change Is the Constant Companion of Progress

When in the wilderness, it's important to stay open to change in your life. We cannot have progress without change. Often, people sincerely want progress, but they don't want to accept change. Picture in your mind progress holding hands with change. What happens is that people beckon progress into their life. They pray for progress. They say, " I want progress." Then as progress approaches, they begin to see the attached changes that come with that progress and refuse change. Progress says, "I'm sorry, I can't help you unless you accept my partner, change. Everywhere I go, he goes."

To reach your full potential in life, you must make friends with change. See change as a positive thing and welcome it into your life. None of us would feel right about a son or daughter who was still in diapers at the age of six. We want to see change! In that realm, we have come to realize that change means progress. When God gets ready to take you to a new level in life, you have to accept change. Along with your promotion, there will come some changes. Reject the changes and you lose the promotion.

Not All Changes Bring Progress but All Progress Brings Change

A common error people make when God is leading them to higher ground, is to avoid making the crucial and proper change. They sense God beckoning them to greater things, but they substitute wrong changes for right ones. The wrong changes are simply changes that do not bring maturity and growth. For example, when it's time to lose weight, it's important to know what to stop eating and what to start eating. If you just change from fried fish to fried potatoes, you won't lose weight. You made a change, but you didn't make the right one.

The people of Israel tried to change everything else but their wrong attitudes. They blamed the leaders, one another, God and anything else they could think of for their lack of progress. Many people get in the wilderness and think, "I must change my church, my job, my spouse, my clothes . . . " Usually, they try to change everything other than the thing God is wanting them to change.

- ◆ Single people think the answer is being married
- ◆ Married people think the answer is being single
- ◆ Blacks blame whites for their problems and whites blame blacks
- ◆ Leaders blame followers and followers blame leaders
- ◆ The government blames the people and the people blame the government

The key to proper change begins within us. This kind of change brings progress along with it.

Faith for the Future

Another thing that happens to people in the wilderness is that they face a strong temptation to go back to the past, rather than having faith for the future.

> Forget the former things; do not dwell on the past. See, I am doing a new thing! Now it springs up; do you not perceive it? I am making a way in the desert and streams in the wasteland.
>
> Isaiah 43:18-19

Life has no rewind button. What *was* is not what should be now, if you are living a life of progress. Your children are growing, your body is changing, people around you may come and go—but God is with you today and will be with you tomorrow. Have faith for the future!

5

THE AUTHORITY TEST

The Authority Test comes to prove your respect for the authority that God has put in your life.

In every worthwhile endeavor of society, there is a genuine need for an authority structure. In some instances, it may be known as a chain of command and in others, a flow chart. Regardless of what it's referred to, it is the solution to chaos, lawlessness and poor organization.

Developing a Proper Attitude toward Authority

The Authority Test will always reveal your attitude toward the authority figures in your life. If you struggle with those people telling you what to do, the test will reveal it. If you resent those over you, the test will reveal it. If you despise those in authority having privileges that you don't have, the test will reveal it. To pass the test we must focus our attention, not on the errors of those in authority, but on our attitude toward authority. More often than not, when we want to change authority, God is wanting to change our attitude toward authority. Our greatest test involving authority comes when we disagree with authority. As long as our authorities do everything like we want it done, there can be no testing of our respect for authority. Therefore, we must observe our attitude most when we don't understand or agree with the decisions and actions of those in authority. I can almost hear the outcry of some: *"But what about bad authority or corrupt leadership? Are you telling me I have to submit myself to authority even when authority is wrong?"*

I hope to answer some of these questions in this chapter. However, I must remind you that there have always been "bad authorities" and always will be. The issue is not them; the issue is you. The goal must be to develop a proper attitude toward authority that is not changed by people in authority, good or bad. Three things that can help us develop a proper attitude are listed below.

1. An awareness of authority

A proper attitude toward authority begins with an awareness of authority. Locate those in positions of authority in your life. Have you accepted them as authorities? Do you admit that they have positions, which place them in authority? Do you find yourself reluctant and trying to be "equal" with them? Only when we are willing to locate them and identify them can we move forward into the place of accepting and respecting their authority. Let me help you consider some areas where authority should exist in your life.

1. In your family
2. In your career/job
3. At your church
4. At your school
5. In your community

As you consider these areas where authority should exist, take note of your attitude. Is it difficult to acknowledge authority in these cases? We can improve attitudes toward authority only after we locate and accept authority.

2. To experience what it's like to be in and under authority

> For I myself am a man under authority, with sol-
> diers under me. I tell this one, 'Go,' and he goes; and
> that one, 'Come,' and he comes. I say to my servant, 'Do
> this,' and he does it.
>
> Luke 7:8

The centurion is assuring Jesus that he understands if Jesus cannot personally come to pray for the sick servant. He is saying, "I know about delegating others to handle respon-sibilities when you have many who need you." Sometimes, I wish as a pastor that all of our congregation realized that one pastor cannot and should not do all the works of min-istry in a church. Some people expect one man to be able to do it all. The following describes the attitude of some:

> He preaches exactly twenty minutes and then sits down. He condemns sin, but never hurts anyone's feelings. He works from 8:00 A.M. to 10:00 A.M. in every type of work, from preaching to taxi service. He makes sixty dollars a week, wears good clothes, buys good books regularly, has a nice family, drives a good car and gives thirty dollars a week to the church. He also stands ready to contribute to every good work that comes along. He is twenty-six years old and has been preaching thirty years. He is tall and short, thin and heavyset, plain-looking and handsome. He has one brown eye and one blue, hair parted in the middle, left side straight and dark, the other side wavy and blonde. He has a burning desire

to work with teenagers, and spends all his time with the older folks. He smiles all the time with a straight face, because he has a sense of humor that keeps him seriously dedicated to his work. He makes fifteen calls a day to church members, spends all his time evangelizing the unchurched and is never out of his office. He is truly a remarkable person...and he does not exist.

I thought you might enjoy that. Back to the point. The centurion's respect and experience for authority caused him to say, "It's okay, Jesus, if you can't come. If you can just speak the word or send someone, I know what it is to say to someone 'go' and he goes." I have found it helpful to experience both sides of authority. Only when you can say, "I know what it's like to be in and under authority," can you genuinely appreciate the blessings of authority. Only when you've been in authority can you relate to those in authority. I find that one who has been in responsible places of authority, generally will be less critical of others who are doing their best in responsible positions of authority. Only after having our own children and assuming responsibility for them do we understand why our parents did what they did.

As a youngster, I often questioned my parents' actions and decisions. I have found that the older I get, the smarter they get! It's easier to understand once you are "there." Until you are a manager, you won't fully appreciate the skills of management. Until you oversee others, you'll never understand the challenge of doing so. Until you lead or govern, you'll have a limited perspective of what it's like to be in authority. Likewise, if and when you are in authority, don't forget what it's like to be under authority. The best leaders use the experiences they had while under authority to help them be better while in authority.

3. To accept God's Word concerning authority

The Bible is absolute in its command that we accept and respect authority. Let's look at a few key Scriptures:

> *Everyone must submit himself to the governing authorities, for there is no authority except that which God has established. The authorities that exist have been established by God.*
>
> Romans 13:1

> *Wives, submit to your husbands, as is fitting in the LORD. Husbands, love your wives and do not be harsh with them. Children, obey your parents in everything, for this pleases the LORD. Fathers, do not embitter your children, or they will become discouraged. Slaves, obey your earthly masters in everything, and do it, not only when their eye is on you and to win their favor, but with sincerity of heart and reverence for the LORD.*
>
> Colossians 3:18-22

> *Obey your leaders and submit to their authority. They keep watch over you as men who must give an account. Obey them so that their work will be a joy, not a burden, for that would be of no advantage to you.*
>
> Hebrews 13:17

The following are Bible words which describe a proper attitude toward authority:

Submission—surrendering, obedience, resignation

> *Everyone must submit himself to the governing authorities...*
>
> Romans 13:1

Respect—to show consideration, honor or esteem for

> *...should consider their masters worth of full respect...*
> 1 Timothy 6:1

Obey—to carry out orders, to be guided by

> *Obey those who rule over you...*
> Hebrews 13:7 (KJV)

Honor—to respect greatly, to show high regard for

> *Give everyone what you owe him...if honor, then honor.*
> Romans 13:7

Below are Bible words which describe a wrong attitude toward authority:

Rebellion—a defiance or opposition to authority

> *For rebellion is like the sin of divination...*
> 1 Samuel 15:23

Sedition—the stirring up of discontent, resistance or rebellion against the government or authority in power

> *Now the works of the flesh are manifest, which are these...seditions...*
> Galatians 5:19-21 (KJV)

Railer—one who speaks bitterly with complaint, aimed at or against something or someone

> *Do not keep company, if any man that is called a brother be a railer...*
> 1 Corinthians 5:11 (KJV)

Insurrection—a rising up against established authority, inclined to be less visible in nature than rebellion

> *Hide me from the secret counsel of the wicked; from the insurrection of the workers of iniquity.*
>
> Psalm 64:2 (KJV)

Recognizing Legitimate Authority

1. Legitimate authority is based on the balancing of privilege with responsibility.

This revelation is especially important to all who reach for "equality" and resist the leadership of others. Let me explain this by giving a couple of examples:

Example A:

If you have two daughters, one fifteen and the other five, the fifteen-year-old should have responsibilities that your five-year-old doesn't have. She also should have privileges that the five-year-old doesn't have. If they are home alone, a natural authority should kick in. As a parent, you should be able to expect the fifteen-year-old to be responsible for the safety and care of the five-year-old. However, unless the fifteen-year-old also has some privileges of authority, she should not be held responsible. Unless you can tell the five-year-old, "Big sis is in charge. Listen to her and obey her," it would not be fair to hold big sis responsible when the five-year-old didn't clean her room, put away toys or go to bed on time. If big sis is ultimately held responsible, she needs the privilege of making the decisions in the house that evening.

Example B:

In business organizations, the owner is responsible for the profits and losses. If you work for a company that can't pay its bills, the collector doesn't come to you, he goes to the ownership. The owner signs documents and legal papers that name him as the individual responsible for the company. Often owners invest everything they have in starting a company. So, it's only fair that they have the privilege of decision making. It's their privilege to not do what an employee may want them to do. It doesn't make them an abusive authority if they make demands on employees without accepting their demands. That's their privilege. It's not inappropriate, nor should it cause offense. It's the privilege that comes with responsibility.

The owner of the company where you work may not have office hours. That's his privilege. He lives with the overall responsibility twenty-four hours a day, seven days a week.

In Numbers 12, Miriam and Aaron sought the privileges of Moses when they had not been given the responsibilities of Moses. God's response was heated, to say the least. He went to great length to explain to them that they were not in an equal place of responsibility and therefore, they did not have the privilege of speaking as Moses spoke.

A few times in my ministry, especially when our church was smaller, somebody would come along and want me to give them speaking privileges in our church. They seemed to feel that since they were attending our church, if they claimed to be called to ministry, I should let them speak in our services. I've heard the same sound that Miriam and Aaron made on more than one occasion, "What makes you so special that you should speak all the time? I'm also called into ministry and should be heard." What these people did not understand was that I was not selfishly hoarding the pulpit at our church. I had been given responsibility to lead and feed the church. I must answer to God for the ministry to the people. Along with that responsibility was the privilege to be the consistent and clear voice to the people. God made me responsible to minister to the needs of the people, and the decision of who should speak was my privilege to choose. Legitimate authority is not responsibility without privilege. Nor is it privilege without responsibility.

2. Legitimate authority is functional authority.

Authority should always have a functional purpose. When there is authority, just for the sake of authority, it ceases to be legitimate. Authority that does not have a functional purpose is dictatorship. It's power driven not purpose oriented. It exists to flex its muscles and exercise power over others. Functional authority exists to accomplish a purpose. It can be short term or long term, but once the purpose is accomplished the authority ceases to exist. Examples of functional authority:

A. A stewardess on an airplane is giving instructions to sit down and fasten your seat belt. Her authority is necessary for safety while on board the plane. Once you exit the airplane, her authority ceases to have a functional purpose.

B. A teacher in a classroom is telling our children how to behave. His authority is necessary for the students to learn. When school is over, the teacher's authority no longer has a functional purpose.

C. A police officer is ticketing a speeding motorist. His authority exists to keep the streets safe and vehicles at a reasonable speed. That's the purpose for his authority. If he exercises authority outside that functional purpose, his authority ceases to be legitimate.

3. Legitimate authority is delegated authority.

Authority does not cease to be legitimate simply because it is received from a higher authority.

- A manager's authority is usually received from an owner or higher authority
- Parents may delegate authority to a baby-sitter
- A pastor may delegate authority to other pastors and leaders

Jesus acknowledged Pilate's God-given authority as legitimate, even though it would not work in His interest.

Jesus answered, 'You would have no power over me if it were not given to you from above.'

John 19:11

He is not denying Pilate's authority; He is acknowledging it as God-given or God-delegated authority.

For those who are in positions of delegated authority, remember that delegated authority should always represent the best interest of those in higher authority. Delegated authority should guard against seeking its own interest when in conflict with those over them. People who don't work as hard when their boss is not around, are not seeking the best interest of the company they work for. Whatever level you're at in an authority structure, recognize your need to fulfill the goals of those you work for. A baseball team has several coaches and one manager. The pitching coach, batting coach and third base coach should all adapt their coaching to the strategies and approach of the manager. Some managers want to play fast-paced, risky baseball. The coaches should pass that philosophy on to the players. The coach, as a delegated authority, should coach according to the manager's philosophy at all times. If he has a differing strategy than the manager, the players must never hear it. He is a delegated authority whose role is to be an extension of a higher authority. His authority is legitimate and should serve the interest of a higher authority.

For those who delegate, remember that although delegating is the passing on of responsibilities, delegation never relieves you of responsibilities. Because you delegate something does not mean you are no longer responsible for it being accomplished. Often young managers or leaders will try to excuse failure by saying to a higher authority, "I gave it to so-and-so to do and they didn't do it," as if to say, "It's not my fault. Don't blame me." Those who accept responsibility eventually have more responsibilities, while those who avoid responsibility eventually have less responsibility. Jesus said, "If you want to be great, learn to serve." In other words, accept responsibility. Those who accept responsibility will grow in greatness.

Passing The Authority Test

When authority fails, our attitude towards authority will be revealed. The failure may be:

- A wrong decision by someone in authority
- A moral failure by someone in authority
- Immature actions by someone in authority
- Unfair treatment by someone in authority
- Discrimination by someone in authority

All of these are obvious failures of integrity, wisdom, character and maturity. However, in Bible examples where authority failed, God still focused his attention on the reactions of those under that authority. He repeatedly let it serve as a time of testing, closely observing their response to the failed authority.

Example A: Genesis 9

Although Noah's conduct was wrong, his failure became a test for his sons. Both obedience and rebellion were revealed.

Example B: 1 Samuel 26

Although Saul was wrong, David said, "Who can touch the Lord's anointed and be guiltless?", thus proving to God his ability to grow in character, not in criticism, when dealing with a failed authority.

It's important to focus on what God wants us to learn when we see the errors of those in authority. The ability to respond properly and without rebellion is the purpose of the test. *There is always a right response to wrong authority.* When authority makes demands on you that are in violation of your conscience, there is a right response. When authority is abusive toward you, there is a right response. When authority extends beyond its functional purpose, there is a right response. The right response can never include a physical or verbal attack on authority The right response can never include a demonstration of anger or hostility. The right response can never be to stir up strife against authority by railing on authority to others. The most common right responses to wrong authority are simple and few. Let me give you two.

1. Appeal to a higher authority
2. Peaceful withdrawal from the authority's jurisdiction or sphere of power

6

THE WARFARE TEST

The Warfare Test occurs when you are in the will of
God and are experiencing problems. This test will
prove how you respond to adversity.

*If they face war, they might change their minds and
return to Egypt.*

Exodus 13:17

*What we accomplish in life is not based on what we
want, but on how much we want it.* One undeniable
ingredient that helps to determine our personal potential
is our capacity to fight for what we want. At a young age,
I was tremendously inspired by a speech Winston
Churchill gave to the British Parliament on June 4, 1940.
With his country under attack from a powerful German
army, he stood boldly before his countrymen and
declared:

> We shall go on to the end, we shall fight in France,
> we shall fight on the seas and oceans, we shall
> fight with growing strength and growing confi-
> dence in the air, we shall defend our island what-
> ever the cost may be, we shall fight on the beaches,
> we shall fight on the landing grounds, we shall

fight in the fields and in the streets, we shall fight in the hills; we shall never surrender...

Winston Churchill

The Threat of War

Many dreams are forsaken at the threat of war. Enemies threaten our marriage, families and integrity. The very thought of confrontation makes most people feel queasy with fear. The two most common fear responses to the enemy's threats are:

1. Ignore the enemy and hope he goes away.

To ignore the enemy is not the same as resisting the enemy.

Resist the devil, and he will flee from you.

James 4:7

Resistance of the enemy is a strategy of war that refuses to surrender territory. For example, in the fight of good against evil, we can refuse to give our attention to something that we sense is either a planned distraction or is simply unworthy of our attention. This strategic resistance is a legitimate strategy of war, but should not be confused with the fearful ignoring of an enemy's presence. To ignore an enemy of your God-given dreams is a weak response to the threat of war.

2. Negotiate and compromise with the enemy.

Samson, a warrior of great potential, got into a compromising position with Delilah. The fear of losing her caused him to negotiate his strength away. With his strength, he lost his vision and ultimately compromised his own destiny.

Every person who has experienced any level of success, will quickly realize that yesterday's success can become tomorrow's failure. Success is an ongoing journey. The career, marriage, the newborn baby all must have today's wisdom and skill to be healthy and strong. We congratulate people when they have a child, but real congratulations are due after they fought off all the threatening forces of evil that attempt to lay hold of the child's life and future. It's not nearly as great to have children as it is to raise them to be Godly, responsible adults.

Likewise, we will face battles that test devotion, perseverance and character when attempting any worthwhile endeavor. Whether raising children, building a business or keeping a marriage happy, we must fight the enemies of excellence.

Picture Your Enemy As Your Footstool

The LORD says to my Lord: "Sit at my right hand until I make your enemies a footstool for your feet."
Psalm 110:1

This powerful message of victories to come was spoken by retiring King David as he passed the scepter of kingship to his son, Solomon. The confidence is obvious as he speaks a prophetic command and promises the desired outcome of his enemies becoming his footstool. What a word-picture to plant in the mind of a new king! It was the picture of absolute, ongoing victory over every foe. He could see all enemies being eventually underneath his authority and power. *It's impossible to pass the test of war with a picture of defeat in your mind.*

The picture in our mind is powerful and self-fulfilling. It is a product of our beliefs, both fear and faith. We've all heard people, after an undesirable experience say, "I knew this would happen." What we don't often realize is that our belief that it would happen probably contributed to it happening. If you picture your marriage falling apart long enough, it eventually will. If you picture yourself not having enough money to enjoy life, you will fulfill that view of your future. On the other hand, people who see their marriage as happy and long-lasting will flow in the direction of that mind-picture. Likewise, people who ponder wise investments and picture a successful financial future, tend to flow in that direction and experience the picture.

The Most Common Enemies We Must Conquer

1. The enemies of mental, emotional, spiritual and physical health

- Unbelief
- Anger
- Low self-esteem
- Sickness
- Negativity
- Bad eating, drinking, smoking habits
- Unhappiness
- Drug abuse
- Hopelessness

2. The enemies of covenant relationships with God, family, church and friends

- Boredom
- Jealousy
- Anger
- Pride
- Lack of consideration
- Lack of motivation

- Weakness
- Sex outside marriage
- Selfishness
- Poor self-image
- Criticism
- Lack of character or integrity
- Injustice
- Misunderstandings
- Lack of honor
- Inconsistency

3. The enemies of prosperity

- Laziness
- Carelessness
- Excessive debt
- Hoarding attitude
- Poor credibility
- Failure to plan
- Ignorance
- Lack of goals
- Failure to honor God with tithes and offerings

The Heart of a Champion

A person with a lot of inner strength is commonly described as having "a lot of heart." The Warfare Test will reveal the level of your inner strength and perseverance.

When the Houston Rockets won their second consecutive NBA title, their head coach was interviewed after the victory, and he had a message for those who had underestimated his team, "Never underestimate the heart of a champion." His message was clearly directed at all of the analysts who tend to look at things like size, speed and talent, but overlook passion, perseverance and the will to win.

The Choice of a Champion

Your potential to conquer will be given many opportunities to prove itself through the course of a lifetime. Champions come in all sizes, shapes and colors. They face adversity in all of its various forms. They are not the "lucky" or "trouble-free" people. Champions are the overcoming people. It's not a result of where they are born, where they go to school, or what happens to them in life. The primary ingredient in the life of a champion is the choice to be a champion.

1. The choice to be a champion empowers a person with the will to win.

To be or not to be, that is the question. Until the question is answered, our will to win is on hold. Ask yourself, "What do I really want to do?" Now ask yourself, "Have I really decided to do it against all odds and whatever it takes?" This could be anything from losing weight to succeeding in business. When you decide and make a definite choice to do something, the will to accomplish it is given direction. Our will is a powerful force waiting to receive direction. The more definite your direction is, the greater your willpower. *An undecided person cannot tap into the strength of his will.* For example, some people are not sure if they are able to serve God or not. They say they want to, but are not sure that they can. The question is not, "Can I do it?" the question is "Have I decided to do it?"

> *But if serving the LORD seems undesirable to you, then choose for yourselves this day whom you will serve, whether the gods your forefathers served beyond the River, or the gods of the Amorites, in whose land you are living. But as for me and my household, we will serve the LORD.*
> Joshua 24:15

Many couples have not decided yet to have a happy marriage. The question is not, "Can we do it?" the question is "Have we decided to do it?" Others have not decided to break the cycle of poverty off of their life. The question is not, "Can I do it?" the question is, "Have I decided to do it?" Once we make a decision, then our will to win (perseverance) can begin to move us toward our goal. We all have something we want to be a champion over. We lack willpower, however, until we make the choice to be champion.

2. The choice to be a champion is an acceptance of God's Word, which says you are a champion.

The choice to be a champion lacks credibility if it is based on always feeling like a champion. I don't always feel like a champion or behave like a champion. My choice to be a champion is not a result of my earning the title of a champion. We may lose battles, but according to God's Word, the believer cannot lose the war. We are destined to win.

No, in all these things we are more than conquerors through him who loved us.

Romans 8:37

...for everyone born of God overcomes the world. This is the victory that has overcome the world, even our faith.

1 John 5:4

People who hesitate in making a choice to be a champion are people who are looking at their own weakness. They see all of their failures. But champions accept God's Word that declares us forgiven, justified, ("just as if I'd never sinned") and righteous before God. This acceptance of God's Word will cause us to reign in life like a champion.

The Most Important Ingredients of a Champion

Some things are not necessary to become a champion fighter. Your formal education, family background, nationality, or hair color—none of those things matter; however, there are two essential ingredients to be a champion fighter.

1. The ability to take a punch—to get hit, even knocked down, and continue to keep fighting.

2. The ability to give a punch—to attack and weaken the strength of the enemy, eventually bringing the enemy down.

Anyone who has watched professional boxing has, no doubt, seen winners whose faces were disfigured from the punishment dished out on them by their opponent. Between rounds, he goes to his corner and they work on his swollen eyes, bleeding nose and busted lip. Then the bell rings and he's back on his feet and into the fight. The ability to take punishment is essential to being a champion fighter. Everyone who "steps in the ring" will eventually get hit hard. If you are afraid of getting hit, you won't be a champion. Champions overcome the fear of the fight and position themselves face to face with the challenge. Champions have the potential to take the best their opponent is able to dish out and continue to keep fighting.

> *We are hard pressed on every side, but not crushed; perplexed, but not in despair; persecuted, but not abandoned; struck down, but not destroyed.*
> 2 Corinthians 4:8

A champion has to take a punch, but he has to do more than be a punching bag. He must have the ability to give a punch, to counterattack, to fight back. When the bell rings, signaling that another round is going to begin, there's no time to nurse those wounds. There's an enemy who has challenged you, taunted you, beckoned you, like the giant named Goliath asking David for a fight. You cannot turn away from it this time. You cannot ignore the challenge; there's too much at stake. It's for your family, your marriage, your future. Fight the fight, come out swinging, don't stop short of feeding his carcass to the fowls of the air. He may be a giant, but this is your chance to be a champion.

7

THE OFFENSE TEST

The Offense Test will come to prove that you are not easily offended and that you have the potential to readily forgive others.

Make every effort to live in peace with all men and to be holy; without holiness no one will see the Lord. See to it that no one misses the grace of God and that no bitter root grows up to cause trouble and defile many.
Hebrews 12:14-15

The word "offense" in the New Testament Scriptures (Matthew 18 and Luke 12) comes from the Greek word, "scandalon," which refers to the method used to ensnare animals in biblical times. First of all, a pit was dug, then covered with branches to camouflage it. Meat, which served as bait, was placed on top of the branches, directly over the pit. As the hungry prey would approach the meat, the branches would cave in, landing the hunter's prey in the pit. The safety of the hunted animal was dependent upon its ability to sense the trap and to avoid it. The free lunch, to satisfy its cravings, was difficult to resist. The trap was designed by the hunter, to be enticing enough to lure its victim in. The only way the animal could avoid its own eventual death was to sense its own fate and free itself from the trap. The hunter, on the other hand, was counting on the animal's inability to resist temptation.

Such is the nature of offenses. It's easy to be drawn into the snare of offenses. In fact, they are designed to lure us in, captivating our attention and causing us to be unaware of the consequences. When an offense comes, you may reason that you have a right to be offended. You may think that any normal person would be upset. You have a cause for anger and hurt. All of that may, in fact, be true. What we usually fail to realize, however, is that when we allow ourselves to enter the mental and spiritual state of being offended, we suffer personal harm.

Who's Responsible?

"So, who's responsible for my not being offended? Is it the people I work with, go to church with or live in the same house with? After all, if they do everything they should do, I won't be offended, right?" Let's consider something together:

+ Did Jesus do everything right?
+ Were people offended by Him?

The answer to both questions is yes.

All ye shall be offended because of me this night...
Matthew 26:31 (KJV)

He was doing what he was supposed to do and people were being offended. The fact is that most people are offended far too easily. I've had people, on numerous occasions throughout the years of my leadership, say to me, "You offended me." What they were really saying was that they wanted me to take responsibility for the fact that they were offended. Even though I may have said or done something they didn't like, that doesn't mean I had said or done anything wrong. While I am responsible for my words, actions and decisions, I cannot be responsible for how others choose to react to them. *In fact, my experience has been that some people have attempted to manipulate others by being overly sensitive and easily offended.* This is how they control their environment and the people in it. They avoid unwanted tasks or confrontation by being so "touchy" that others are expected to accommodate them. Many people go through life like this. Instead of taking responsibility for not being offended, they hold others responsible to not offend them. Eventually, this offense trap takes people away from healthy, happy relationships and the freedom to enjoy life. This may mean that you have to overlook the behavior of other people that could be offensive. Sometimes, it's words that would have been better left unsaid. Other times, it's a lack of consideration for your feelings. Whichever the case, you will live a happier life by deciding to overlook it. The same goes for the times when the behavior is intentional. Learn to overlook it. By doing so, you keep yourself out of the offense trap.

A fool shows his annoyance at once, but a prudent man overlooks an insult.

Proverbs 12:16

...it is to his glory to overlook an offense.

Proverbs 19:11

Offenses Will Come

The opportunity to be offended will present itself repeatedly in your life. Unfortunately, many people are looking for it rather than overlooking it. The prejudices of gender, race, age and status present plenty of opportunities for offenses. In fact, any time you socialize or have contact with other people, opportunities for offense are inevitable. Below are some relationship principles to help you avoid the offense trap.

1. Define accurately your role in the relationship.

Roles are necessary to maintain order and avoid chaos in life. However, if roles are unclear, the people involved are more vulnerable to offense. When you look at your relationships, accept the importance and value of everyone's roles, rather than ignoring them. With those roles come responsibilities and privileges. Relationship roles, common in most of our lives include the following roles of:

- Fellow human beings, who are strangers
- Friendships
- Employer/employee
- Law enforcement officials
- Siblings
- Parents
- Children
- Mentors
- Spouse
- Fiancée
- Leader
- Counselor
- Overseer or manager
- Pastor

Treat everyone with whom you're acquainted with dignity and respect. Going beyond that, be conscious of their role in your life and yours in theirs. If you are experiencing tension or conflict in a relationship, it's possible that someone involved is not considering or respecting the roles in that relationship.

2. Assume the best about others.

Give people the benefit of the doubt. Believe that they mean well or have good intentions, even when you don't understand their actions. Cynicism is the belief that other people's actions are wrongly motivated. Since we are incapable of knowing men's hearts, it's always good to assume the best rather than risk judging them falsely. This keeps you from offense when you don't understand someone's actions.

3. Meddle not.

Don't involve yourself in other people's affairs unless you are invited. It's not the act of helping other people that we are avoiding, rather the act of seeking information and creating conversation in other people's matters.

> Like one who seizes a dog by the ears is a passer-by who meddles in a quarrel not his own.
> Proverbs 26:17

> Make it your ambition to lead a quiet life, to mind your own business, and to work with your hands.
> 1 Thessalonians 4:11

Our sphere of concern is usually larger than our sphere of influence. To avoid offending and being offended, we should concentrate on and stay within our sphere of influence. For example, you may have a friend who confides in you about his or her troubled marriage. They may disclose secrets that their spouse would not want you to hear. Rather than forming an opinion based on one side of the story, encourage your friend to go to a profession-al counselor or minister and get help. If you're not a coun-selor, don't try to be one. The best thing a friend can do is continue to be a friend and not meddle in other people's matters. Your sphere of influence is in being a friend. Even as a pastor, I'm slow to get involved with people's lives unless I'm certain that I should. There are always factors to consider; don't just rush in.

4. Never use a relationship to manipulate or control a person.
It sounds like this:

+ "If you loved me you would..."
+ "If you cared about my feelings you wouldn't..."
+ "If you want us to remain friends..."

When people act out of obligation or demands imposed on them by others, rather than their own desires, they grow to resent it. Sometimes people don't actually speak their expectations of others. They imply those expec-tations through behavior, in order to get the desired response from the other person. This form of manipulation is effective on people who are afraid of losing a relation-ship. They do things to please the person, even when it's not what they want to do. Offense is an inevitable destina-tion when you travel this road. Good friends don't impose their preferences on friends. Good husbands and wives seek the other's interests above their own.

5. Don't expect more out of a relationship than can come forth naturally and organically.
Offense comes when we "keep score" in a relation-ship. It's always a one-sided perspective and sounds like this:

- "I called you last time, it's your turn."
- "She didn't even speak to me. I was right there, and she walked right by."

When a person gets stubborn and decides to ration their relationship efforts, they have given place to offense. *It is impossible for an offended person to have healthy, enjoyable relationships.* You can keep offense at a distance by realizing that relationships must come naturally. It cannot be forced or pushed into existence. That doesn't mean you can't facilitate relationships by making calls, planning fellowship, etc. But you must always allow it to unfold.

If you or someone else does otherwise, offense is sure to follow. The same is true when passing through the season of relationships. It will not always be as it used to be, or as it is going to be. There are seasons to relationships. If you don't flow with it, you risk offense.

The Trap Is Also a Test

An opportunity for offense is not only a trap, it is also a test. God observes us during the hard and difficult times of our lives. The ability to rise above feelings of hurt or resentment and genuinely forgive others is followed by Godly promotion in our lives. *There is a difference in a temporary feeling of offense and a mental and spiritual state of being offended.* The temporary feeling of offense may happen before you realize it. There are times when it will be unavoidable. The state of being offended, however, is what happens when you do not make the choice to free yourself of the offense. Signs that you are moving into a state of being offended are:

- Incidents consume your thoughts
- Incidents affect your sleep

- You find yourself daydreaming about the incident
- You have growing feelings of anger and resentment about the incident
- You find yourself doing things that prove you are not getting over the incident (leaving your church, telling someone off, desiring to get even)

Matthew 18 describes the two sides of an offense. Verse six clearly pronounces woe upon those who offend others, intentionally or carelessly. Verses seven and eight are an extreme caution against allowing yourself to be offended.

> *If your hand or your foot causes you to sin, cut it off and throw it away. It is better for you to enter life maimed or crippled than to have two hands or two feet and be thrown into eternal fire.*
>
> Matthew 18:8

I hear Jesus saying, "Do whatever you have to do. Go to drastic measures and extreme decisiveness to avoid offenses in your life." So many people today are living miserable, lonely lives because they allowed themselves to fall into the trap of offense. It doesn't help to be bitter. **You can't change what has happened, but you can change how you are responding to it.** You can decide today that you will "flush out" all those wrong feelings you have and free yourself of offense.

You see, the passing of an offense test happens when you have reason to be offended, but you refuse the opportunity. The greater your ability to not be offended, the more God can use you.

> *Great peace have they which love thy law: and nothing shall offend them.*
>
> Psalm 119:165 (KJV)

The people who choose to live without offense will enjoy great peace. Offenses pile up within some people to the point that they have no peace. These people are troubled in mind and spirit. But the people who live without offense have great and lasting peace in their life. I decided that people would have to work hard to offend me. If you want to offend me, it's going to have to be a deliberate and serious offense. And my plan, even then, is to get over it!

8

THE TEST OF TIME

The Test of Time comes to prove the quality of your patience and your confidence in God through the seasons in your life.

Let us not become weary in doing good, for at the proper time we will reap a harvest if we do not give up.
Galatians 6:9

Time affects people differently. Some people are like milk, they get bitter with time. Others are like wine, they get better with time. The "milk" people have a short life span of:

- Interest—they are easily distracted
- Motivation—they run out of inspiration quickly
- Confidence—their attention gets turned toward the negative
- Determination—they start well but never finish

Great ideas will always turn sour in the mind of a milk person. Great opportunities repeatedly curdle for a milk person. These people have not allowed time to work to their advantage. As soon as something is familiar, they begin to lose appreciation for it. Whether it's a job or a new relationship, milk people do well as long as something is "new" to them. Over time, however, things for them have a tendency to spoil. This loss of interest and appreciation soon leads to inconsistencies and their enthusiasm dwindles until, of course, something new comes along. Then the process is repeated.

The Unfolding of Your Potential

We cannot reach our full potential without time. On Valentine's Day every year, florists around the nation are searching for roses that are at the "unfolding" stage. These flowers must be given time to open. You cannot speed up the process by grabbing the rose pedal and pulling it open. To do so is to risk permanent damage to an otherwise "perfect in its own time" rose. The proper use of time is essential, if the rose is going to reach its full potential. Not only can the process not be rushed, but the rose needs specific forms of nurturing while in the process. The atmosphere, the soil and the water are all contributing to the maturity and unfolding process of the rose. People are much the same way. In order to achieve our full potential, not only do we need nurturing, we also need the proper amount of time. To some, however, time is of no benefit. These people don't grow. They don't mature, they don't make progress. These are the people who fail The Test of Time. I'm not referring to a time management program (although that may be a helpful tool along the way); rather, I'm referring to the proper use of life's opportunities and circumstances.

A Window of Time

Life is God's gift to me—what I do with it is my gift to God. Most people get so distracted with the urgent matters of daily living that they neglect the important matters of a lifetime. The urgent matters press in on us—things like changing the oil in the car, balancing the checkbook and picking up the dry cleaning. The important matters of a lifetime only reveal themselves periodically. Concerns for building a strong family, preparation for eternity, physical health or sufficient financial resources seem to emerge less often. It may come to our attention when we hear of close friends who are getting divorced, attend a funeral or experience a financial crisis. It's in those moments of life that we may purpose to give more attention to our own relationship with God, our family or commit to a financial growth plan for our future. However, the best things in life are not free, they require our time and efforts. Simply wishing for the things that matter most in life will cause a person to never know them as reality in their life.

Life's best opportunities are within a window of time.

- The opportunity for education
- The opportunity to spend time with your children
- The opportunity to teach your children
- The opportunity to increase wealth
- The opportunity to be a young man or woman of God
- The opportunity to choose a career
- The opportunity to learn from a lesson
- The opportunity to know certain people better
- The opportunity to thank certain people
- The opportunity to honor your parents
- The opportunity to plan financially for retirement
- The opportunity to prevent health problems in your future
- The opportunity to love your spouse and build a happy relationship with them

Passing The Test of Time means that we seize the opportunities of a lifetime while we have the "open" window.

It's OK to Want

Delight yourself in the LORD and he will give you the desires of your heart.

Psalm 37:4

One of the reasons some Christians don't make the proper use of time is that they are indifferent to their own desires. They spend a lifetime suppressing the desires of their heart, rather than allowing those desires to inspire them to greatness. There are desires born of our flesh that will hinder us from a life of worth and value. There are also desires in our heart that are given by God to guide us into our destiny. When a person suppresses all their desires, they "lose their way" in life. When David said, "the LORD is my shepherd, I shall not want" some people may think he was renouncing his own desires. In reality, however, he was proclaiming the Lord's promise of provision in his life, that his want would be satisfied. Some of life's best opportunities, listed above, may be in the top ten want list for your life. Giving yourself the green light to be inspired by your wants can help you make the proper use of your time. Once you are convinced that it's okay to want, there are three other strategies that will cause your wants to be a product of your time.

This strategy has to do with prioritizing your wants. It takes you beyond an admission of many wants and forces you to declare what you want the most. It's easy for all of us to be taken off course from the things that are most important to us. If a boat leaves Seattle headed for Hong Kong, the captain must continually adjust its course based on wind, waves and other conditions. To be only slightly off course en route can become hundreds of miles off course over the length of the journey. The captain must continually monitor the ship's course and not allow the ship to drift out of line with his desired destination. The same is true in our lives. We must be focused on the things that we want most. Slight variations of our energy and time today can make a big difference on where we arrive ten years from now. Knowing your priorities and keeping them in daily focus will help to keep you on target with your desired destination. To do this, priorities should periodically be reprioritized.

This strategy has to do with planning the journey from where you are to where you want to be. The three most common errors of planning are listed below with a reference of Scripture.

Mistake #1—To have no plan

This is a "whatever will be will be" mentality rather than a "whatever will be is influenced by me" mind-set. How can you hit a target that does not exist? It's common for people to not have a plan to reach their desired destiny, which may be the reason so few do.

> *But the noble man makes noble plans, and by noble deeds he stands.*
>
> Isaiah 32:8

Mistake #2—To not include others while planning

Most people are willing to include others in their planning, but don't know how. Two bums were sitting on a park bench discussing their ill fate when one said, "I'm sitting here because I listened to nobody." The other one replied, "I'm here because I listened to everybody." When you include others in your planning process, it's important to use their counsel wisely and with discretion. Wisdom is usually found in the collection of various thoughts consolidated together rather than in one individual's advice. Your unique situation is not a carbon copy of anyone's previous situation. Realize that, collectively, your advisers help you plan wisely.

> *Plans fail for lack of counsel, but with many advisers they succeed.*
>
> Proverbs 15:22

Mistake #3—To not include God when planning

Again, I don't think it's a matter of not *wanting* to—but a matter of not knowing *how* to include God that hinders most people. This mistake is addressed in the writings of James.

> *Now listen you who say, 'Today or tomorrow we will go to this or that city, spend a year there, carry on business and make money.' Why, you do not even know what will happen tomorrow. What is your life? You are a mist that appears for a little while and then vanishes. Instead, you ought to say, 'If it is the Lord's will, we will live and do this or that.'*
>
> James 4:13-15

The teaching here is not against a plan for tomorrow, but rather an emphasis to plan and include God in the plan. Notice again that verse 15 tells us to proclaim our plans for tomorrow while leaving room and staying flexible for God's will to be accomplished.

We have to have a plan, first, before we can commit our plans to the Lord. How do you commit a plan to the Lord if the plan does not exist? Including God in our plans will cause our plans to succeed.

Commit to the Lord whatever you do, and your plans will succeed.

Proverbs 16:3

Seeking what you want, through planning, is another important key in the proper use of time. Most of us have had to sit in meetings that did not have a planned agenda. Inevitably, little if anything was accomplished. We've all experienced a difference in learning when a teacher plans for the class versus "flying by the seat of their pants." In those situations, nobody likes to feel they are wasting their time. The big picture of life must be planned also, if time is valuable enough not to waste it.

This strategy has to do with our perspective. Periodically, it's important to get a new improved perspective in one or more areas of our life.

- Perspective of our self
- Perspective of our spouse
- Perspective of our church
- Perspective of our career

Since there's always more than one way to look at everything, chances are that even as you read this line, you are in need of a better, more God-like perspective in one or more areas of your life. An important key to happiness is not only getting what you want, but wanting what you get. To be continually aware that:

- I *want* my family
- I *want* this day
- I *want* my career
- I *want* my church
- I *want* my marriage
- I *want* this challenge

This ability to want what you have can be lost by looking through the lens of bad experiences, frustration or personal weariness. The new perspective of genuine appreciation for what you have is the perspective of those who are champions in life. These people pass The Test of Time by not allowing their blessings to become so common that they fail to recognize and appreciate them.

Think Long Term

People who pass The Test of Time are people who learn to think long term. These people greatly consider how their thoughts, words, actions, behavior and choices will affect them long term. Parents, for example, sometimes allow their children to do things that are funny or cute when they are infants, not realizing that those same things are embarrassing and ugly in later years. Employers sometimes drop quality standards to be nice to an employee, not realizing that a random act of kindness can evolve into a major compromise of quality and an erosion of excellence over time. Long-term thinkers are careful to not start a pattern today that they don't want as a habit tomorrow.

There are some things about you that only time can prove. The lesser quality clothes get worn out quicker. The lesser quality paint fades faster. The higher quality trucks last longer. Stamina and endurance are traits of people who are strong and in good shape. Our quality, our strength and our full potential is revealed in The Test of Time.

Dealing with Disappointment

Greg Norman, otherwise known as "The Shark," is one of pro golf's most talented and celebrated player on today's circuit. Although he was the top money winner in

1995 or years gone by, he has never won a major tournament on American soil. He has developed a reputation for not winning the big ones from repeatedly (seven times) placing second in these major events. In the 1996 Masters, at Augusta, Georgia, it appeared he would change that by finally winning the prestigious Masters title. He shot some of the best golf ever played in the history of Augusta, for the first three days of the tournament. On the last and final day, disaster hit his game and he recorded what is perhaps the biggest disappointment in golf history. Sports programs, newspapers and magazines made it the headline story for several days, saying things like "Norman folds," Norman "chokes" etc...

Because he is so popular in the golfing world, people everywhere were feeling sorry for him. It would have been understandable if he had felt sorry for himself. Everyone would have accepted Norman as only being "normal" if he had refused to speak to media, expressed self-doubt or neglected to compliment others who had played well that day. But Norman is not "normal," he's a class "A" champion golfer. On the day of the big disappointment he showed the courage and optimism that got him to where he is today. In his postgame interviews, he spoke with ease and confidence. He was gracious, kind and saw beyond the present disappointment. In fact, his words were inspiring. Here's some of what he said...

> I'm a winner. I lost today, but I'm not a loser in life. I've won golf tournaments. There's people who would want to win as many as I have....maybe the things I have done to myself are for a reason. Maybe something really good is waiting to happen to me down the road. This is just a test.
>
> Greg Norman
> April 14, 1996

How we handle disappointment is crucial in The Test of Time. It makes some bitter and some better. Never allow a disappointment to steal the joys of life. *As hard as the disappointment may feel today...it may very well be the test you must pass, en route to a greater tomorrow.* The sum of our life is not a result of what happens to us, but rather how we deal with it. Deal well with disappointment and time will be on your side.

9

THE LORDSHIP TEST

The Lordship Test occurs when you are in a position or situation where you must choose to obey God over your natural instincts.

Do not let this Book of the Law depart from your mouth; meditate on it day and night, so that you may be careful to do everything written in it. Then you will be prosperous and successful.

Joshua 1:8

To Pass This Test
I Must Believe That God Is Always Right

When I invited one of our neighbors to church recently, He stated his plans for his daughter's future. He said that he intended to send her to a variety of religious services while she was young, so that she could develop an openness towards all beliefs. As he shared his philosophy with me, my mind flashed to my teenage days when my own mother warned me that, "If I became too open-minded there was a danger that my brain would fall out." Although this neighbor thinks he is doing his daughter a great favor, I could not help but feel how unfortunate it was that she would not receive clear and definite spiritual guidance from her father. Let's be reasonable...

- What if he approached her education the same way?
- What if he let her choose her behavior and provided no guidance?
- Why not let her decide which foods to eat after taking a sample taste of all of them?

If he did this, could he expect more than an uneducated, misbehaving, unhealthy child? Unfortunately, unless there is a change, this daughter will have a weak, undeveloped faith in God. Her future will have "absolutes" in other areas but be void of understanding and direction in the ways of God. One of my greatest rewards as a teacher is to see people get answers to their questions about life. It's exciting to watch people discover that biblical principles "work." In our ministry, people often approach us with personal testimonies of powerful transformations after deciding to do things God's way. You see, human tendency will often guide us in a different direction than God would guide us.

A verification of His Lordship in our lives is our belief that God is *always* right. It's inconceivable to us to think of buying a new automobile and ignore the instructions of the owner's manual. To disregard these important guidelines for operation and maintenance would threaten our safety and jeopardize the condition of the vehicle. In fact, most warranties are valid based on the owner's observation and adherence to the manual. *The Bible is the owner's manual of life.* A dedicated observation and adherence to its instructions will bring maximum results. **When people disregard or pay no attention to God's guidelines, they lose the benefit of God's guarantee on life.**

To Pass This Test
I Must Be Willing to Obey God's Instructions for My Life

Obedience is much easier when we realize the benefits of obedience. Wise parents, for example, teach their children to realize a connection between actions and consequences. To get this connection established in the mind of a young child, parents must reward proper behavior and punish improper behavior. The hope of the parent is that the child realizes that there are consequences for their actions. To fully realize this is to be equipped to make good choices in life.

One of our ministry slogans is "Success Begins On Sunday." When people first hear us say that, they may wonder what success and Sunday have in common. Most people are inclined to think success is something that happens Monday through Friday...but Sunday? The office, the school, that sales meeting, the interview...that's what most people think of as the beginning place for success. Our message is that genuine, lasting success has it roots in the knowledge and obedience of Bible principles. You can have a good education and a great career and still never know real success. Bible principles will give you a proper perspective on all of the important issues of life—God, family, marriage, finances...to name a few. Bible principles will also help you to develop right attitudes, which are essential to happiness. When it comes to success, there is no substitute for obedience to Bible principles.

I've often daydreamed of what it would be like if every person in the world agreed to live by the principles of the Bible for just one week. Imagine a world where everyone is honest, thankful, productive...no violence, cheating, hatred or strife. No babies conceived out of wedlock, no DWIs, drunkenness or suicide…what a great place to live! We may never convince everyone to live by this standard, enjoying all its benefits, but we can experience the personal and family benefits of a godly lifestyle. The greatest of all benefits for obedience, however, is the promise of God's blessing upon our lives.

If you fully obey the LORD your God and carefully follow all his commands I give you today, The LORD your God will set you high above all the nations on the earth. All these blessings will come upon you and accompany you if you obey the LORD your God.
Deuteronomy 28:1-2

You will be blessed in the city and blessed in the country.
Deuteronomy 28:3

The fruit of your womb will be blessed…
Deuteronomy 28:4

…and the crops of your land and the young of your livestock—the calves of your herds and the lambs of your flocks. Your basket and your kneading trough will be blessed.
Deuteronomy 28:4-5

The LORD will grant that the enemies who rise up against you will be defeated before you. They will come at you from one direction but flee from you in seven.
Deuteronomy 28:7

The LORD will send a blessing on your barns and on everything you put your hand to. The LORD your God will bless you in the land he is giving you....The LORD will grant you abundant prosperity—in the fruit of your womb, the young of your livestock and the crops of your ground—in the land he swore to your forefathers to give you. The LORD will open the heavens, the store-houses of his bounty, to send rain on your land in season and to bless all the work of your hands. You will lend to many nations but will borrow from none.

Deuteronomy 28:8, 11-12

A Blessing Release—Not a Blessing Bribe

Some people's concept of God's promise to bless obedience is shallow and contrary to God's nature. Here's a typical example of what goes on in some people's minds when they hear that God will bless them if they obey: "Is this God's way to get me to do what He wants—offer me a 'blessing bribe'? If God loves me, why doesn't He bless me regardless of what I do?" These people have failed to understand that God does not withhold blessing from anyone. God did, however, create the physical and spiritual universe to respond favorably to corresponding action. The Bible is simply the instruction manual that informs us of what kind of behavior is "blessed" and what kind of behavior is "cursed." For example, when I tell my daughter to eat right and she will feel good or warn her of how bad she will feel if she eats chocolate bars all day, I'm teaching her to comply with a truth that applies to her. I'm not bribing her to get what I want; I'm instructing her so she can get what she wants. The outcome is predictable based on how she decides to eat. Likewise, our obedience to the Bible is our obedience to God's knowledge regarding the laws of the universe. We all have the opportunity to see blessings released in our life as a result of a corresponding action.

Due to technology, many of us can walk up to a machine thousands of miles from home, push a code of numbers and get cash to drop from the machine. The machine is not prejudiced against, our race, age, lifestyle or appearance. If you push the right numbers, the machine will release a blessing! Without the right numbers, however, you can stand there all day and scream, holler, complain or get mad, but you won't get cash. In much the same way, *God created the universe to respond with blessings upon the individual whose actions command the release of them.* God has established this without any prejudice. He is no respecter of persons, but has given everyone the opportunity to live a life of blessing.

Put Your Obedience Where Your Mouth Is

Now a man came up to Jesus and asked, 'Teacher, what good thing must I do to get eternal life?' 'Why do you ask me about what is good?' Jesus replied. 'There is only One who is good. If you want to enter life, obey the commandments.' 'Which ones?' the man inquired. Jesus replied, 'Do not murder, do not commit adultery, do not steal, do not give false testimony, honor your father and mother,' and 'love your neighbor as yourself.' 'All these I have kept,' the young man said. 'What do I still lack?' Jesus answered, 'If you want to be perfect, go, sell your possessions and give to the poor, and you will have treasure in heaven. Then come, follow me.'

Matthew 19:16-21

Although this young man declared his obedience to the commandments, he faced The Lordship Test when Jesus said, "Go and sell everything you have and give it to the poor." Jesus' intention was not to strip him of his wealth, but to prove his potential to be obedient to God. The rich young ruler had virtually said, "I've kept all the commandments from my childhood up. I've kept the law of God. I love the Lord with all my heart, mind and soul." So Jesus replied, "Okay, if that's true, go and sell everything you have and give it to the poor." In my words He was saying, "Put your obedience where your mouth is."

I believe it's possible that if the young man would have said, "Yes, Sir," and turned to walk away, Jesus would have let him travel about ten steps before stopping him to say, "Young man, come back here. Now that I know your heart, you don't really have to do that." This is what happened with Abraham and Isaac. When Abraham raised up the knife to thrust into Isaac's young body, the angel stopped him and said, "No, no, no! It's not your son that God wants." God just wanted to know that the rich young ruler loved Him enough to obey Him, even when it pertained to his money. Many people, who claim Jesus as Lord, have failed to put their obedience where their mouth is. As soon as they hear a Bible principle taught that they don't want to follow, they simply disregard it. This person will often continue to profess the Lordship of Christ while failing to obey his teachings.

The Lordship Test is the opportunity to prove our trust in God's ways and thoughts as being greater than our own.

'For my thoughts are not your thoughts, neither are your ways my ways,' declares the Lord. 'For as the heavens are higher than the earth, so are my ways higher than your ways, and my thoughts than your thoughts.'

Isaiah 55:8-9

Next time you face a decision in life, ask yourself, "What would God's thoughts be on this matter?" It's quite encouraging when you become aware of your own ability to receive God's wisdom for life. It's exciting to know that we can tap into "higher thoughts" and "higher ways." With all of the confusion and failure around, why not accept instruction from the Creator himself? As we accept God's guidance in various areas of our life, we are sure to experience promotion and enjoy success.

The Lordship Test Requires You to Trust Him

One of my lifelong dreams was to hunt a Dahl sheep in Alaska. These sheep are considered one of the most challenging big game trophies in the world. They exist only in Alaska and British Columbia and are elusive to hunters, hanging out in the open high country. Without any real pursuits of this desire, God opened the door and I jumped at the opportunity. The odds of my having any success in a hunt of this magnitude would be next to impossible without a guide. The value of a guide became even more obvious after my plane landed and I began to journey into Alaska's vast open wilderness. Because my "guide" was also a good friend and member of the church, I never had a doubt in his ability to provide accurate guidance and direction on my journey. He knew the country like the back of his hand. When he told me to do something, I did it. When he said, "This is when we get up," I got up. When he said, "This is the horse you should ride," I got on. When he said, "Stay ready for grizzlies," I said, "Absolutely." When he said, "Turn right and head through the canyon," he got no argument from me. I elevated his guidance for the entire week. I could have sat at home and never went to Alaska, pondering on whether I could trust my guide. I could have questioned everything he said to do, and we would have never made progress. But I decided to trust his guidance completely and "Yes" I had the ultimate success. As good as God's guidance is, it will be of no value to you until you decide to trust it. When you abandon your own thoughts to believe His, then He can guide you.

Trust in the Lord with all your heart, and do not lean on your own understanding. In all your ways acknowledge Him and He will make your paths straight.

Proverbs 3:5-6

Trust is the key to Lordship. He will guide you through life, if you trust Him!

What Is Your Decision?

If you have never received Jesus Christ as your personal Lord and Savior, why not do it right now? Simply repeat this prayer with sincerity:

"Lord Jesus, I believe that you are the Son of God. I believe that You became a man and died on the cross for my sins. I believe that God raised you from the dead and made you the Savior of the world. I confess that I am a sinner, and I ask you to forgive me, and to cleanse me of all my sins. I accept your forgiveness, and I receive You as my Lord and Savior. In Jesus' name, I pray. Amen."

...if you confess with your mouth, 'Jesus is Lord', and believe in your heart that God raised him from the dead, you will be saved. For it is with your heart that you believe and are justified, and it is with your mouth that you confess and are saved...for, 'Everyone who calls on the name of the Lord will be saved.'

Romans 10:9, 10, 13

If we confess our sins, he is faithful and just and will forgive us our sins and purify us from all unrighteousness.

1 John 1:9

Now that you have accepted Jesus as your Savior:

1. Read your Bible daily—it is your spiritual food that will make you a strong Christian.

2. Pray and talk to God daily—He desires for you to communicate and share your life with him.

3. Get planted in a local church where you can grow in knowledge and be equipped to live an overcoming Christian life.

4. Let your light shine by your good works so that others will see God better by looking at you.

Please let us know the decision you made.

AUTHOR CONTACT INFORMATION

Kevin Gerald Communications
c/o Champions Centre, home of
Covenant Celebration Church
1819 E. 72nd Street
Tacoma, WA 98404

www.kevingerald.com